ULTIMATE COMFORT FOOD

Si King & Dave Myers
THE HAIRY BIKERS

ULTIMATE COMFORT FOOD

Food, love & comfort

We've all got to eat to stay alive, but food is so much more than nourishment. Good food is a pleasure, it's creative – and it's comforting. Food means home. Food can bring back memories of childhood, of special occasions, of good times. Some of us – and we're mentioning no names – wake up thinking of what to cook and eat and then go to sleep at night planning the next day's meals.

Cooking great food is also about showing and sharing love. What could be a nicer way of showing you care than making a beautiful meal for those special people in your life? But also, when you're on your own, there's nothing better than putting together something tasty to give yourself a bit of a treat. Whether you're cooking up a fab feast for Sunday dinner with the family or making supper for one to have on a tray in front of the telly, you'll find something to enjoy in this collection of recipes.

At times like these when money is tight and life a bit stressful, good food can be a cuddle for your soul as well as your belly. We made a TV series called 'Comfort Food' a while back and catching some repeats of the show got us chatting. We started thinking how great it would be to explore the idea of comforting cooking in more depth. So here we are. And never has writing a book made us feel so hungry and keen to get in the kitchen and cook!

It's important to say that comfort food isn't all about buttery bakes and hearty pies and stews. They play a part certainly, particularly on cold winter days, but you need comfort in all seasons, in sunshine and showers, and a tasty ham and potato salad or a light fresh fennel and white bean soup can bring cheer at any time of year. And it's not just about British staples. In the years we've been cooking together we've travelled the world and found little gems to gladden our hearts and tickle our taste buds everywhere from Shanghai to Southampton.

We've come up with some twists on old favourites as well as some brand-new ideas in the following pages. For instance, we both love a risotto, and we agree that spaghetti carbonara is high on the comfort food chart, so we've combined the two to make risotto carbonara – something we hope will become a new go-to favourite. It really is a big hug of a dish. We just had to include a shepherd's pie in our book and this one is a bit special – a duck confit shepherd's pie which you're going to love.

The following pages are packed with ideas for quick snacks, midweek suppers, weekend specials and tempting teatime treats and puds. It's food that's all about love and generosity, food that makes you feel glad to be alive. We're thrilled with these dishes, and we think you will be too, so head to the kitchen and get comfy!

Some tips from us

Peel onions, garlic and other veg and fruit unless otherwise specified.

Use free-range eggs whenever possible. We reckon that 95 per cent of good cooking is good shopping – great ingredients need less fussing with – so buy the best and freshest that your budget allows.

Weigh all your ingredients and use proper measuring spoons and jugs. This is particularly important with baking recipes.

We've included a few stock recipes at the back of the book and home-made stock is great to have in your freezer. But if you don't have time, you can find some good fresh stocks in supermarkets or you can use the little stock pots or cubes.

Every oven is different, so be prepared to cook dishes for a shorter or longer time, if necessary. We find a meat thermometer is a useful bit of kit to help you get perfectly cooked meat and chicken. They are readily available online and in kitchen shops.

Dave
x

Everyone has their own childhood memories of favourite foods. In our house, Monday was washing day and baking day. My mother would make bread, a Victoria sandwich cake, fruit scones and light, pillowy, floury baps. I still remember the smell of those baps fresh out of the oven and I love them to this day. When I started to learn to cook, Friday was stay-up-late night and a chance for me to make my own supper. I'd be given a couple of potatoes to make chips and I'd put them in a good old-fashioned chip butty. That sense of comfort was sublime.

Passions change and develop over the years and later on when I came to London for college I was knocked out by all the new and exciting foods I discovered. Best of all was getting back to my little flat and having a chicken madras and pilau rice!

Nowadays, Si and I realise we're some of the luckiest men on Earth, with the travels we've made and the food we've eaten. From slurping down bowls of ramen in Yokohama to munching cheesy chips on the prom on the Isle of Man after a day's TT racing, it's all been magnificent. We've loved every minute of our journey in food.

I've always loved my food. My dad was in the Navy and used to arrive home from his travels bringing exotic ingredients like star anise and lemon grass – unknown in Kibblesworth, our little pit village on a windswept hill the northeast. Stella, my mam, was an amazing cook and early on in life I realised our food wasn't quite like that of other families. Mam was really ahead of her time in the way she used an array of herbs and spices to create mouth-watering curries and comforting casseroles on a limited budget. I loved it all.

For me, food means joy and nostalgia. The smell of a favourite dish immediately takes me back to memories of being sat round a table enjoying a meal with family or friends, to thoughts of love, kindness and togetherness.

And that's what this book is about – a collection of what we think are the most comforting recipes in order to celebrate the importance of food in our lives and the joy and satisfaction it can bring. We hope you enjoy them as much as we do.

soups
& stews

Fennel & white bean soup

Serves 4

1 tbsp olive oil
15g butter
1 large onion, finely chopped
1 large fennel bulb, finely sliced
pinch of sugar
2 garlic cloves, finely chopped
½ tsp fennel seeds
2 bay leaves
100ml white wine
100g cherry tomatoes, puréed
2 x 400g cans of cannellini beans
    (500g cooked beans)
1 litre vegetable or chicken stock
salt and black pepper

To serve
squeeze of lemon juice
chilli flakes (optional)

We love a bean soup and this one is light and fresh but still really velvety and comforting. Kingy loves cooking with fennel and it really does bring this soup to life. If you fancy giving the soup more of a kick, sprinkle a few chilli flakes over each bowlful. And we suggest puréeing just a few ladlefuls and leaving the rest as it is to give a nice mix of textures.

Heat the olive oil and butter in a large saucepan. Add the onion and fennel and sauté them over a medium-high heat until both start to take on some colour. Add a pinch of sugar and continue to cook until the veg are lightly caramelised, then stir in the garlic, fennel seeds and bay leaves. Season with salt and pepper.

Pour over the wine and bring to the boil. Turn down the heat, cover the pan and leave the onion and fennel to braise gently until completely tender.

Add the cherry tomatoes to the pan and cook for a couple of minutes before stirring in the beans and stock. Bring to the boil, then turn the heat down and simmer gently for 15 minutes.

Take out the bay leaves, then remove a few ladlefuls of soup and purée lightly in a blender. Tip the purée back into the pan, stir and heat through again.

Ladle the soup into bowls and add a squeeze of lemon juice. Have some chilli flakes to add at the table if you like.

Tomato soup with cheesy dumplings

Serves 4

1 tbsp olive oil
25g butter
1 large onion, finely chopped
½ sweet potato, peeled and diced
3 garlic cloves, finely chopped
½ tsp ground cinnamon
1 large tarragon sprig
1 large basil sprig
2 x 400g cans of chopped
    tomatoes
500ml vegetable or chicken stock
pinch of sugar (optional)
50ml single cream (optional)
salt and black pepper

Dumplings
125g breadcrumbs
½ tsp baking powder
75g hard cheese (Parmesan or a
    very mature Cheddar), grated
1 tsp mustard powder
1 tsp dried oregano
1 egg
50g ricotta or cream cheese

To serve
25g Cheddar cheese, grated
a few basil leaves

My mam used to serve canned tomato soup with fried cheese sandwiches. This is a refined version and if I do say so myself, twice as tasty as my mother's was and a bit better for you – it's nice and not so naughty. We've added sweet potato, a pinch of cinnamon and some herbs for extra deliciousness and who doesn't love a dumpling? A perfect combo, I think. (Dave)

Heat the olive oil and butter in a large saucepan. Add the onion and sweet potato and cook them gently over a gentle heat until the onion is soft and translucent. Add the garlic and cinnamon, stir for another minute or so, then add the herbs, tomatoes and stock to the pan. Season with plenty of salt and black pepper.

Bring to the boil, then turn the heat down, cover the pan and leave to simmer for 20 minutes. Remove the tarragon and basil, then blitz the soup until smooth, using a hand or jug blender. Taste for seasoning and add a pinch of sugar if necessary. You can also add the cream at this stage if you think the soup needs it.

While the soup is simmering, make the dumplings. Put all the ingredients in a bowl and season with plenty of salt and pepper. Mix thoroughly and form into 8 balls. They will seem quite firm at this stage.

Drop the cheesy dumplings into the soup and cover the pan. Simmer for about 10 minutes until the dumplings have swelled a little and are cooked through. Serve the soup garnished with a sprinkling of cheese and a few basil leaves.

French onion soup

Serves 4

75g butter
1kg onions, thinly sliced
    (about 3mm is good)
leaves from a large thyme sprig
large pinch of demerara sugar
    (optional)
1 tbsp plain flour
150ml dry sherry or white wine
1 tbsp sherry vinegar
1 bay leaf
850ml stock (beef, chicken
    or vegetable)
up to 1 tbsp brandy
salt and black pepper

Croutons
8 rounds of baguette
1 garlic clove, halved
butter, for spreading
100g Gruyère cheese, grated

You don't have to be on a skiing holiday to enjoy this soup! One of the great classics, French onion is one of the most warming soups imaginable. Up to you what stock you use. If you're veggie, go for vegetable, but we like chicken or a mixture of chicken and beef. The trad way of finishing this is to put the bowls of soup with the cheese-topped croutons under the grill, but we favour this slightly easier method of grilling the croutons first, then adding them to the soup. That way you get a nice mix of browned cheese and melting, stringy, soft cheese in the bowls.

Melt the butter in a large saucepan, add the onions and thyme leaves and stir to coat them. Put the lid on the pan and leave the onions to cook for about 10 minutes over a low heat until they have softened.

Turn the heat up to medium and cook the onions until caramelised – this is not a fast process and will probably take at least an hour, perhaps longer. A fair amount of liquid will evaporate off first, as the onions release water and lose volume, then they will slowly brown. Stir them regularly, scraping up the brown layer which will coat the base of the pan. Add a splash of water from time to time if the onions are getting close to burning. Taste when you think they are caramelised enough and add a pinch of sugar if they need any additional sweetness.

Stir in the flour and cook it for a couple of minutes or so to get rid of the raw flavour. Add the sherry or white wine and bring it to the boil, stirring constantly to deglaze the base of the pan. Add the sherry vinegar, bay leaf and stock, then season with plenty of salt and pepper.

Bring the soup to the boil again, then turn down the heat, partially cover the pan and simmer for about 45 minutes. Add the brandy, a teaspoon at a time, stirring it in and tasting until you are happy with the flavour. Check for seasoning at the same time and adjust as necessary.

Heat a grill. Toast the baguette slices, rub them with the cut garlic and spread with butter. Divide half the cheese between the croutons and grill until the cheese has started to brown, then pile the rest of the cheese on top. Serve the soup with the croutons.

Pasta & chickpea soup

Serves 4

2 tbsp olive oil
1 large onion, finely diced
1 large carrot, finely diced
2 celery sticks, finely diced
3 garlic cloves, finely chopped
leaves from a large rosemary sprig,
    finely chopped
1 tsp dried oregano
2 bay leaves
2 x 400g cans of chickpeas
200g canned or fresh tomatoes
800ml vegetable or chicken stock
100g small soup pasta
salt and black pepper

To serve
squeeze of lemon juice
handful of parsley, finely chopped
pinch of chilli flakes

This is a riff on the Italian pasta e ceci – *pasta and chickpea stew. A beautifully tasty, hearty bowlful, this really does warm the cockles and is a meal in itself. We've opted to keep this recipe veggie and it's fab, but you could add some diced bacon, pancetta or chorizo if you like.*

Heat the olive oil in a large saucepan and add the onion, carrot and celery. Sauté over a medium heat until the onion and celery are translucent and all the vegetables are tender. Turn up the heat a little so the veg take on some colour, then stir in the garlic. Cook for another couple of minutes, then add the herbs, chickpeas, tomatoes and stock. Season with salt and pepper.

Bring to the boil, then turn the heat down, partially cover the pan with a lid and leave to simmer for about 15 minutes. Remove the lid and add the pasta. Cook until the pasta is just the soft side of al dente, then taste to check the seasoning and adjust as necessary.

Add a squeeze of lemon juice and serve with a sprinkling of parsley and some chilli flakes for a touch of heat.

Clam chowder

Serves 4

1 tbsp olive oil

100g smoked bacon lardons

25g butter

1 onion, finely diced

400g floury potatoes, diced

2 celery sticks, diced

2 leeks, cut into slim rounds

2 bay leaves

1 thyme sprig

1 tbsp plain flour

400ml chicken or fish stock

1 x can or jar of clams (about
    300g, undrained weight)

200ml milk

squeeze of lemon juice (optional)

salt and black pepper

To serve

handful of parsley, finely chopped

crusty bread

This is so good. There's something lovely about a chowder and for this recipe we've kept things really easy by using clams from a can or jar – cheaper than fresh and you can keep some in your store cupboard. The clams usually come in a light brine or clam juice which you can use as part of the cooking liquor, but we advise tasting it first to make sure it isn't too salty. As is traditional, this chowder is thickened with potatoes, which gives it a really comforting texture.

Heat the olive oil in a saucepan and add the bacon. Fry until crisp and brown, then set it aside on kitchen paper to drain.

Add the butter to the pan. When it has melted, add the onion, potatoes, celery and leeks. Sauté for a few minutes over a medium heat until they are all glossy with butter and starting to turn translucent, then add the herbs. Stir in the flour – it should make a paste around the vegetables – then pour in a little of the stock. Stir thoroughly to make sure the flour has completely combined without going lumpy, then add the rest of the stock.

Strain the clams over a bowl, taste the liquid and add it to the pan if it tastes good. Season with salt and pepper as needed. Bring the soup to the boil, then turn the heat down and simmer for about 15–20 minutes until the vegetables are tender.

Put the bacon back in the pan and add the clams and milk. Don't let the soup come to the boil again – just simmer it gently until piping hot. Taste for seasoning again and add a squeeze of lemon juice to cut through the richness if you think it necessary. Garnish with parsley and serve immediately with some good crusty bread.

Ham hock & red lentil soup

Serves 4

1 small ham hock, smoked
    or unsmoked
½ onion
6 cloves
3 bay leaves
large thyme sprig
a few allspice berries

Soup

2 tbsp olive oil
1 onion, finely chopped
2 carrots, finely diced
2 celery sticks, finely diced
3 garlic cloves, finely chopped
300g red lentils, well rinsed
1.2 litres ham stock
1 hot chilli pepper (optional)

To serve

1 tbsp olive oil
100g reserved ham hock,
    shredded
1 tbsp light brown soft sugar
1 tsp hot sauce (optional)

A ham and lentil soup tops the comfort charts for us – and for most people we think. We both loved our mothers' versions and this is ours – could it be even better? Ham hocks are cheap to buy from your butcher or supermarket and there's quite a bit of meat on them which you could use for the salad on page 64. If you don't want to cook a ham hock, you could add a ham bone to the soup or just use a ham stock cube.

If cooking a ham hock from scratch, check first whether it needs soaking. If it does, either soak it overnight in cold water, or use this quick method: put the ham hock in a large saucepan and cover it with water. Bring to the boil and leave it for 2 minutes, then drain thoroughly. Give the ham and the saucepan a wash to get rid of any starch, then put the ham back in the pan.

To cook the ham, put it in a large pan, cover it with water and bring to the boil. Skim off any foam until it starts turning white instead of mushroom-coloured. Stud the onion with the cloves and add it to the pan along with the herbs and allspice berries. Turn down the heat and simmer for 1½–2 hours until the ham is cooked and tender.

Remove the ham from the pan and strain the liquid, discarding the aromatics. When the ham is cool enough to handle, remove the meat from the bone, discarding the skin and fat as you go.

To make the soup, heat the oil in a large saucepan. Add the vegetables and sauté them over a medium heat until they are softened and starting to take on some colour. Add the garlic and continue to cook for another couple of minutes. Stir in the lentils and pour in the stock, then add the chilli pepper, if using. Bring to the boil, then turn the heat down to a simmer. Taste for seasoning and add salt and pepper as necessary – how much salt you need depends on the saltiness of the ham stock.

Simmer until the vegetables are tender and the lentils have broken down completely – this will take 25–30 minutes. Remove the chilli pepper, if using.

To make the garnish, heat the oil in a small frying pan and add the shredded ham hock. Sprinkle over the sugar and hot sauce, if using, then season with salt and pepper. Stir over a medium-high heat until the meat is crisp and lightly caramelised. Serve the soup with a generous sprinkling of ham hock.

Coconut noodle soup

Serves 4-6

1 tbsp coconut oil

3 tbsp Vietnamese curry paste
(see p.257)

3 chicken thigh fillets or 2 chicken
breasts, finely sliced

500ml chicken or vegetable stock

400ml can of coconut milk

2–3 tbsp fish sauce

juice of 1 lime

1 tsp palm sugar or light brown
soft sugar

1 red pepper, cut into strips

120g baby corn, cut in half,
diagonally

200–250g pak choi, trimmed
and halved lengthways

300g flat rice noodles

1 tsp sesame oil

salt and black pepper

To serve

4 spring onions, shredded

handful of coriander, mint
and/or Thai basil leaves

chilli oil

A comforting dish that whisks you away to far-off shores – and you don't need a passport! You do have to make a curry paste for this recipe but once that's done the soup is so quick and easy. Vary the veg according to what you like or have available – for instance, you could add sprouting broccoli instead of pak choi.

Heat the coconut oil in a large saucepan and add 2 tablespoons of the curry paste. Fry until the paste starts to smell aromatic and is slightly caramelised from the sugar, then add the chicken and fry until lightly browned.

Pour in the stock and coconut milk and bring to the boil. Season with salt and black pepper and add 2 tablespoons of the fish sauce, half the lime juice and the sugar. Simmer for a couple of minutes. Add all the vegetables and continue to simmer until they are tender. Taste and add more fish sauce and lime juice to get the flavour you want.

Cook the noodles according to the packet instructions, then toss them in the remaining curry paste and the sesame oil. Divide them between the bowls, then ladle over the soup, making sure the chicken and vegetables are evenly distributed. Garnish with the spring onions and herbs, then serve with some chilli oil on the side.

Chicken soup

Serves 4

30g butter
1 onion, diced
2 large carrots, diced
2 celery sticks, diced
300g potatoes, diced
3 chicken thigh fillets, diced
3 leeks, sliced into rounds
3 garlic cloves, finely chopped
leaves from 4 large tarragon
    sprigs, finely chopped,
    plus extra to garnish
100ml white wine
750ml chicken stock
50ml double cream
salt and black pepper

Many people believe that a good bowlful of chicken soup cures all ills and heartbreaks and we think this recipe fits the bill. There's a bit of chopping to do but when you taste the soup you'll know it's all been worthwhile. With protein, carbs and plenty of veg, this is a delicious meal in itself and very welcome at any time of year.

Heat the butter in a large saucepan and add the onion, carrot, celery and potatoes. Cook for 10 minutes over a gentle heat, stirring regularly, then turn up the heat and add the chicken.

Cook until the chicken is lightly coloured on all sides, then stir in the leeks, garlic and tarragon. Stir for another minute, then pour in the white wine and season with salt and pepper. Bring the boil, cover the pan and leave to braise until the vegetables are tender – this will take about another 10–15 minutes.

Pour over the stock and bring to the boil. Lower the heat and simmer gently for about 10 minutes, then check the vegetables – the potatoes should be breaking up and everything else should be cooked. Stir in the cream and reheat until piping hot. Serve in bowls with a little more chopped tarragon sprinkled on top.

Mulligatawny

Serves 4-6

2 tbsp coconut oil or olive oil
1 large onion, diced
2 large carrots, diced
½ small swede, diced
400g stewing lamb, finely diced
1 tsp mustard seeds
15g root ginger, grated
4 garlic cloves, finely chopped
2 tbsp curry powder
2 tbsp tomato purée
50g red lentils, well rinsed
1 litre vegetable or chicken stock
50g basmati rice
1 red pepper, diced
1 eating apple, peeled and diced
200g curly kale, destemmed and
    shredded
salt and black pepper

To serve (all optional)
sliced green chillies
yoghurt
mango chutney
chopped coriander

A classic soup, this originated in India then became popular in Britain in the 19th century. The name comes from the Tamil words for pepper and water and there are many different versions – not all of which contain meat, which was probably a British addition. It's a great dish, nourishing and warming, and you can take your pick of garnishes – chillies to ramp up the heat, yoghurt to temper it or mango chutney for heat and sweetness. We go for all three, plus a sprinkle of coriander. Like many spicy dishes, this is great in summer or winter.

Heat the oil in a large saucepan and add the onion, carrots and swede. Sauté over a medium-high heat until the vegetables are starting to brown, then turn up the heat, add the lamb. and sear it on all sides. Add the mustard seeds and leave them until they start spitting.

Reduce the heat and stir in the root ginger and garlic. Cook for a couple of minutes, then stir in the curry powder and tomato purée. Stir until the tomato purée starts to separate, then add the red lentils and stock.

Season with plenty of salt and pepper and bring to the boil, then reduce the heat and cover the pan. Simmer for about 20 minutes, until the lentils are well on their way to being tender, then add the rice, red pepper, apple and kale. Continue to cook until the rice is tender – probably another 15–20 minutes. Keep an eye on the liquid levels and add a little more stock if necessary. Check the seasoning and add salt and pepper to taste.

Ladle into bowls and serve with your choice of garnishes.

Beef & barley stew

Serves 4-6

2 tbsp olive oil or dripping

500g braising or stewing steak,
    cut into chunks

1 large onion, diced

2 celery sticks, sliced

2 large carrots, sliced into slim
    rounds

200g swede, diced

3 garlic cloves, chopped

3 tbsp tomato purée

100ml red wine

3 bay leaves

75g barley

1.2 litres beef stock

2 leeks, cut into rounds

½ green pointed cabbage,
    shredded

salt and black pepper

To serve

a few dill or parsley sprigs,
    finely chopped

We're both big fans of barley and think it isn't used enough. A real winter warmer, this stew tastes even better the next day, so make plenty and treat yourself. The sweetness of the leeks and cabbage marry perfectly with the meltingly tender meat to make a truly mouthwatering bowlful of goodness.

Heat the olive oil or dripping in a large saucepan or flameproof casserole dish. When it's hot, add the beef and sear it on all sides, then transfer it to a plate.

Add the onion, celery, carrots and swede to the pan and sauté over a medium heat until they have taken on some colour. Add the garlic and stir for a couple of minutes, then stir in the tomato purée. Continue to stir for another 2–3 minutes until the raw taste of the tomato purée has been cooked out.

Pour over the red wine, bring to the boil and deglaze the base of the pan thoroughly, scraping up any sticky bits. Put the beef and any juices back in the pan and add the bay leaves and barley. Season with plenty of salt and pepper.

Pour in the beef stock. Bring to the boil, then turn down the heat and cover the pan. Leave to simmer for an hour, by which time the beef should be tender and the barley cooked.

Add the leeks and cabbage, pushing them into the liquid, then cook for another 20 minutes or so until they are tender. Check the seasoning, then serve the stew with a sprinkling of dill or parsley.

snacks & light comforts

Tomato monkey bread

Makes 1 loaf

Dough
500g strong white bread flour,
     plus extra for dusting
7g fast-acting dried yeast
2 tsp sugar
1 tsp salt
150ml tomato juice,
     at room temperature
100g sunblush tomatoes,
     at room temperature
2 tbsp olive oil
1 egg

Garlic butter
100g butter, melted
3 garlic cloves, crushed
2 tbsp finely chopped parsley
salt and black pepper

Filling
125g stuffed olives (anchovy
     or pimento), sliced
50g Parmesan cheese, grated
a few basil leaves, finely chopped

To finish
15g Parmesan cheese, grated

*if you don't have a bundt tin,
use a roasting tin or a large
cake tin (25–28cm). To get
a hollow middle, just put
a ramekin or a scrunched-up
ball of foil in the centre for
guidance when assembling.*

Very popular in the States, monkey bread is often sweet and served at breakfast but we like our savoury version. It's fun to make and even more fun to eat. Put this bread on the table and watch it disappear in a flash.

To make the dough, put the flour in a bowl or the bowl of a stand mixer with the yeast and sugar. Stir thoroughly, then add the salt and stir again. Do not add the yeast and salt together without mixing – if the salt comes into contact with the yeast it will inhibit its action. Purée the tomato juice and sunblush tomatoes together until smooth. Add enough just-boiled water to bring their combined weight to 325g.

Add the olive oil and egg to the flour mixture, then gradually work in the tomato mixture. Mix until you have a smooth dough, then knead until the dough is soft and pliable. This will take about 5 minutes in a stand mixer or 10 minutes by hand. The best way to judge whether the dough is ready is the windowpane test. Take a section of the dough and stretch it out as much as you can in all directions. If you can stretch it so thin that you can almost see through it, it's been kneaded enough. Cover the dough with a damp cloth and leave it somewhere warm to rise until it has doubled in size. This will take at least an hour or longer depending on the temperature.

Make the garlic butter. Melt the butter in a small saucepan and add the garlic together with a generous pinch of salt and some black pepper. Set aside.

Lightly dust a work surface with flour, then turn the dough out and knock it back. Shape it into a rough rectangle, then scatter over the olives, cheese and basil, spreading them as evenly as possible. Cut the dough into about 30 squares, then fold the dough of each square around the filling into a ball.

Brush a large bundt or ring tin with some of the garlic butter and arrange the balls in 2 or 3 layers, depending on the dimensions of your tin. Brush with more butter and sprinkle some Parmesan between each layer, reserving a tablespoon of the Parmesan for later. Cover with a damp cloth and leave the dough to prove again, this time for about half an hour.

Preheat the oven to 220°C/Fan 200°C/Gas 7. Sprinkle the remaining Parmesan on top of the bread, then bake for 25–30 minutes until well risen and firm to the touch. Remove the bread from the tin by placing a plate over the top and turning the tin over. Then put a cooling rack over the ring of dough balls and upturn again, so the dough balls are the right way up on the cooling rack. Warm the garlic butter through if it has set, then stir in the parsley and brush generously over the bread balls. Serve warm or leave to cool. Reheat the garlic butter for dipping before serving.

Tiger bread

Makes 1 loaf

500g strong white flour,
    plus extra for dusting
7g fast-acting dried yeast
2 tsp light brown soft sugar
8g salt
30g butter
150ml milk
175ml cool or tepid water

Topping
60g rice flour
1 tsp fast-acting dried yeast
1 tbsp light brown soft sugar
2 tsp sesame oil

A real childhood favourite revisited. We think the pattern on this delicious bread looks more like the markings of a giraffe than a tiger and it comes from a rice flour paste that is painted on to the dough before baking! The recipe originates from the Netherlands and its Dutch name is 'tjigerbrood' – hence it became known in English as tiger bread. This is great slathered with plenty of butter.

First make the dough. Put the flour in a large bowl or the bowl of a stand mixer and mix in the yeast and sugar. Add the salt and mix again. Put the butter and milk in a small saucepan and heat gently until the butter has just melted, then add the water to this mixture. Slowly work the wet ingredients into the dry ingredients until you have a soft, sticky dough. If it's still quite dry, add a little more water.

Cover the dough with a damp tea towel and leave it to stand for half an hour. This will give the gluten a chance to start working and will make kneading easier. Turn the dough out on to a floured surface and knead by hand or with a stand mixer until the dough is smooth and no longer sticky. A good way to check is the windowpane test – stretch out the dough very carefully and if you can stretch it enough to see through it, it's ready.

Put the dough back in the bowl and cover it with a damp tea towel. Leave it to stand for a couple of hours until it has doubled in size. Knock back the dough until it deflates, then knead it a couple more times. Pat the dough out into a large rectangle, then roll it up tightly and form it into an oval loaf. Put it on a baking tray, cover it with a damp tea towel and leave it to prove for about 20 minutes. Preheat the oven to 220°C/Fan 200°C/Gas 7.

Mix together the topping ingredients with 50ml of water to make a smooth paste. After the bread has proved for about 20 minutes, spread it thickly with the paste. Leave it to stand for about another 20 minutes until it is well risen.

Bake in the oven for 25–30 minutes until the bread is a dark golden brown and cracked in that distinctive pattern. Make sure it sounds hollow when tapped, then remove it from the oven and leave to cool before eating.

Garlic bread pizzas

Serves 4

1 large baguette
100g butter, softened
4 garlic cloves, crushed
50g Parmesan cheese, grated
1 tsp garlic powder (optional)
salt and black pepper

Topping
1 tsp dried oregano
150g cherry tomatoes, chopped
200g mozzarella, sliced
1 tbsp olive oil
a few basil leaves

Garlic bread and pizza were two of our favourite things in our student days, so putting them together is a win-win for us. Great for those moments when you fancy a pizza but don't want the faff of preparing dough, these are dead easy to make – a speedy hit of comfort. The garlic powder adds a nice smokiness to the flavour but feel free to leave it out if you don't have any.

Preheat the oven to 200°C/Fan 180°C/Gas 6.

Trim off the ends of the baguette if you like, then cut it in half and split each half lengthways so you have 4 pieces of bread.

Put the butter in a bowl and add the garlic, Parmesan and garlic powder, if using. Season with salt and pepper and mix thoroughly. Spread the butter generously over the bread, then sprinkle over half the dried oregano.

Put the cherry tomatoes in a sieve and sprinkle them with salt. Toss gently and leave to stand for 10 minutes. Arrange the mozzarella over the bread slices, then top with the tomatoes. Drizzle with the olive oil, then add a few basil leaves and sprinkle with the remaining oregano.

Place on a baking tray and bake for about 15 minutes, until the bread is crisp and the cheese is well melted. Enjoy at once.

Cheese toasties with nduja

Makes 4 toasties

8 large slices of sourdough
    or robust bread
mayonnaise, for spreading
150g mature Cheddar, grated
150g good melting cheese, such as
    Ogleshield, Comté or Gruyère
1 red onion, finely chopped
3 medium tomatoes, finely diced
a few watercress sprigs
200g nduja

There's nothing quite as cheering as a good cheese toastie and we think adding some spicy nduja is a genius idea though we say it ourselves. These can be made in a panini-style toastie maker, with flat plates or in a frying pan. These toasties can be a bit messy to eat but they're oh so good.

Take 4 of the slices of bread and spread mayonnaise on what will be the outer side of each. Mix the cheeses, red onion and tomatoes together and divide the mixture between the 4 slices, pressing the cheese down as much as possible. Top with the watercress. Spread the nduja on to one side of each of the remaining slices of bread and place, nduja-side down on the filling. Press the slices firmly together to make sandwiches.

Grill in a panini-style toastie maker until the cheese has melted. Alternatively, cook the sandwiches in a dry frying pan, flipping them until both sides are crisp and golden brown. Lightly covering the pan as you cook the toasties will speed things up a bit.

Cut each sandwich in half and serve immediately. The filling will be volcanic, so be careful!

Devilled eggs

These make lovely little snacks and are perfect for part of a buffet lunch or, if you're feeling a bit fancy, to serve as canapés at a party. Pick your favourite filling or go wild and make all three. An oldie brought up to date by us – and a goodie.

Each of these fillings is enough for 4 eggs

eggs, at room temperature
salt and black pepper

Classic
2 tbsp mayonnaise
1 tsp English mustard
½ tsp hot paprika, plus more
    to garnish
a few drops of red wine vinegar
    or lemon juice
leaves from a small tarragon sprig,
    finely chopped
1 spring onion, very finely
    chopped, to garnish

Curried
2 tbsp mayonnaise
1 tsp Dijon mustard
½ tsp hot curry powder
1 tbsp finely chopped coriander
    (plus whole leaves to garnish)
squeeze of lemon juice
2 green chillies, very finely
    chopped or sliced, to garnish

Capered
2 tbsp mayonnaise
1 tsp Dijon mustard
1 heaped tsp capers, finely
    chopped
1 heaped tsp olives, finely
    chopped
zest of ½ lemon
squeeze of lemon juice
a few small basil leaves, to garnish
chilli flakes, to garnish

Put the eggs in a saucepan and cover them with cold water. Bring to the boil, then turn the heat down to a simmer and cook for 10 minutes. This should ensure that the yolks are completely cooked – they need to be dry and crumbly for devilled eggs.

Plunge the eggs into cold water and as soon as they are cool enough to handle, peel off the shells. Cut the eggs in half and scoop out the yolks. Set the whites to one side and put the yolks into a bowl. Crumble the yolks into a powder – you can do this with a fine grater, or just break them up with a fork, but make sure there aren't any lumps.

For each type of devilled eggs, add all the ingredients to the egg yolks and mix together thoroughly. Taste for seasoning – some of the ingredients are quite salty – and add salt and pepper as necessary.

To fill the eggs, either pile the mixture into the cavity left by the whites – or if you want to be a little more elegant, use a star nozzle with a piping bag and pipe in the filling. Add any garnishes and arrange the eggs on a serving plate.

Stuffed garlicky mushrooms

Serves 4

8 field mushrooms
100g butter
4 garlic cloves, crushed
1 tbsp olive oil
1 shallot or small onion, finely
    chopped
small bunch of parsley, finely
    chopped
leaves from a few tarragon sprigs,
    finely chopped
1 tsp mustard powder
25g Parmesan cheese, grated
60g breadcrumbs
salt and black pepper

Stuffed mushrooms are often overlooked but we find it hard to resist them when we see them on a menu. Super-garlicky and very moreish, these will tickle your taste buds no end. There's plenty of garlic butter in this recipe and we use it to brush the mushrooms before baking and in the filling to give a double hit of flavour. A real treat.

Trim any overhanging bits from the field mushrooms and remove the stalks. Finely chop the trimmings and stalks and set aside.

Melt the butter, then stir in the garlic and season with salt and pepper. Leave the butter to infuse for 5 minutes, then use some of it to brush the tops of the mushrooms. Arrange the mushrooms upside down on a baking tray. Preheat the oven to 200°C/Fan 180°C/Gas 6.

Heat the oil in a small frying pan and add the shallot or onion and the mushroom trimmings. Fry briskly until the shallot is translucent and the mixture is quite dry, then remove the pan from the heat. Stir in all the remaining ingredients.

Reheat the remaining garlic butter if it has set, then pour it over the mixture and stir thoroughly. Divide the mixture between the mushrooms. Bake the mushrooms in the oven for 15–20 minutes until they are cooked through and the topping is golden brown.

Noodle salad

Serves 4

200g rice noodles
1 tsp sesame oil
200g broccoli, shredded
1 large courgette, sliced
100g baby corn, halved
1 red pepper, deseeded and
    finely sliced
½ Chinese cabbage, shredded
1 avocado, peeled and sliced
small bunch of coriander
leaves from a small bunch of mint
leaves from a small bunch of basil
    or Thai basil
salt and black pepper

Dressing
100ml coconut milk
2 tbsp soy sauce
15g root ginger, grated
1 garlic clove, grated
1 tsp hot sauce
zest and juice of ½ lime
generous pinch of ground
    turmeric

We need comforting dishes in hot weather as well as cold, and this noodle salad slips down nicely when there's a heatwave but you still want some cosy carbs. We've kept this vegetarian, although you could add some cooked chicken or prawns or even leftovers from the Szechuan lamb (page 172) or pork belly (page 170). Fry any leftover meat briefly to crisp it up before adding.

First prepare the noodles according to the packet instructions. For wide rice noodles, we usually cover them with freshly boiled water and leave them to stand for 20–25 minutes. When they have softened to the right texture, drain them and run them under cold water. Toss with the sesame oil.

Bring a saucepan of water to the boil. Season with salt and add the broccoli, courgette and baby corn. Cook for 2 minutes, then drain and refresh under cold water. Set aside.

Make the dressing. Whisk all the ingredients together and taste for seasoning. Add salt and pepper as necessary.

To assemble, put all the vegetables – raw and cooked – into a large bowl with the noodles. Pour over the dressing and mix thoroughly. Stir through half the herbs and then garnish the salad with the rest.

Spanish-style roasted vegetables with halloumi

Serves 4

3 aubergines, trimmed and left
　　whole
4 long red peppers
1 red onion, finely sliced
1 tbsp sherry vinegar
3–4 medium tomatoes, sliced
1 large cos lettuce, shredded
2 tbsp capers
leaves from a small bunch of mint,
　　to garnish
salt and black pepper

Halloumi
1 tbsp olive oil
2 x 225g blocks of halloumi, sliced
1 tsp dried mint

Dressing
3 tbsp olive oil
1 tbsp sherry vinegar
1 garlic clove, peeled and left
　　whole

Based on a classic Spanish vegetable dish called escalivada, this aubergine and pepper salad is super-tasty and has a beautifully comforting texture. We like to add some slices of fried halloumi for extra interest and protein. This dish looks as good as it tastes, so a real winner.

Preheat the oven to 200°C/Fan 180°C/Gas 6. Pierce the aubergines all over with a knife tip or skewer, then place them on a baking tray with the peppers. Roast them in the oven for about 45 minutes, until the peppers are blackened and the aubergines have started to collapse and soften.

Put the red onion slices in a bowl, sprinkle them with salt and toss with the sherry vinegar. Leave to stand for half an hour.

For the dressing, whisk the olive oil and sherry vinegar together and season with salt and pepper. Bruise the garlic clove lightly and add it to the dressing. Leave to stand for half an hour.

When the aubergines and peppers are ready, remove them from the oven and put them in a bowl. Cover with a plate or tea towel, then leave them to steam as they cool. When they are cool enough to handle, remove the skin and seeds from the peppers and pull the flesh into strips. Pull the aubergine flesh apart.

Heat the oil in a large frying pan and add the slices of halloumi. Fry them until golden brown on both sides, in batches if necessary, then remove and sprinkle with the dried mint.

To serve, arrange the lettuce on a serving dish or individual plates. Top with the peppers and aubergines and season with salt and pepper. Drain the onion slices and add them and the tomato slices to the salad. Sprinkle over the capers and drizzle over the salad dressing. Finally, add the halloumi and garnish with mint leaves.

Smoked fish salad

Serves 4

300g waxy potatoes (skin on),
  diced
1 large carrot, diced
75g frozen peas
75g green beans, trimmed
  and cut into rounds
1 large cos lettuce, shredded
100g radishes, finely sliced
2 celery sticks, finely chopped
2 tbsp capers, rinsed
2 large gherkins, finely diced
zest of 1 lemon
200g smoked mackerel, pulled
  into bite-sized pieces
small bunch of dill, finely chopped
leaves from a large tarragon sprig,
  finely chopped
salt and black pepper

Dressing
1 small shallot, finely chopped
1 tbsp cider vinegar
1 tsp Dijon mustard
2 tbsp olive oil
2 tbsp soured cream

Smoked mackerel is cheap, available in every supermarket and great for a quick and easy meal. We've added loads of cooked and raw vegetables, plus tasty capers and gherkins, to make this into a real festival of flavours and textures.

First make the salad dressing. Put the shallot in a bowl and sprinkle with salt. Add the cider vinegar and leave to stand for half an hour. Whisk in the mustard, followed by the olive oil, then finally stir in the soured cream. Taste and season with salt and pepper as necessary. Thin the dressing with a little water if it seems very thick.

Bring a pan of salted water to the boil and add the potatoes and carrot. Cook for about 6 minutes, then add the peas and green beans. Continue to cook until everything is just tender, probably for another 2 minutes. Drain thoroughly and leave to cool.

To assemble the salad, arrange the shredded lettuce on plates or on a serving dish. Put the cooked vegetables in a bowl with all remaining raw vegetables, the capers and gherkins and spoon over most of the dressing. Toss gently to coat the vegetables, then add the lemon zest, most of the mackerel and most of the dill and tarragon.

Spoon this mixture over the lettuce, then top with the remaining mackerel, dill, tarragon and dressing.

Prawn & fish balls

Serves 4

Makes 20

200g peeled raw prawns,
    roughly chopped
250g white fish fillet, diced
zest and juice of 1 lime
4 spring onions, very finely
    chopped
1 egg white
40g cornflour
2 tbsp breadcrumbs
olive oil, for frying
salt and black pepper

To coat
25g plain flour
1 egg, beaten
50g breadcrumbs

To serve
lime wedges
tartare sauce (shop-bought
    or see p.262)

Put a bowl of these little beauties on the table and we promise you they'll vanish in no time. They are light and so tasty and the only problem is stopping yourself from eating the whole lot. You can buy tartare sauce, of course, but try making your own from our recipe on page 262 if you have time. These are an affordable alternative to scampi and some people think they're even better. Chips optional!

Put two-thirds of the prawns and all of the fish into a food processor and pulse to a paste. Finely chop the remaining prawns. Put the processed fish and prawns and the finely chopped prawns in a bowl with all the other ingredients, except the olive oil, and season generously with salt and pepper. Mix thoroughly to combine, then put the mixture in the fridge to chill for at least half an hour.

Form the mixture into 20 balls. The easiest way to ensure you get the right size and number is to weigh the mixture and divide it by 20 – each ball should be about 25g.

Put the plain flour into a shallow bowl and season with salt and pepper. Beat the egg in another shallow bowl and put half the breadcrumbs in another. Dip each ball in the flour, followed by the egg and finally in the breadcrumbs. Top up the bowl of breadcrumbs when necessary.

To shallow fry, cover the base of a frying pan with oil and heat to medium-high. Fry the balls for 3–4 minutes on each side until they are a deep golden brown and piping hot in the middle. It's probably best to do this in 2 batches. Drain the balls, on kitchen paper then serve with lime wedges to squeeze over and the tartare sauce on the side.

Savoury egg custards

Serves 4

Filling
oil, for greasing
150g cooked shrimp or prawns
5g root ginger, finely chopped
4 spring onions, finely chopped
1 tsp sesame oil
1 tsp soy sauce
salt

Custard
3 eggs
350–425g dashi or chicken or
    vegetable stock
1 tbsp soy sauce
1 tbsp mirin
1 garlic clove, crushed or grated

To serve
a few coriander leaves
16 stems of asparagus, trimmed
    and steamed

Any kind of custard is a comforting dish and this is our version of a beautiful Japanese-style savoury custard. You can add all sorts of extras, such as cooked chicken, enoki mushrooms or wilted greens, but here we've gone with shrimp or prawns which work brilliantly. These are great with asparagus or just with some buttered toast. Top tip is to keep the water below the steamer simmering very gently. If the heat is too high, the custards can split.

Lightly oil 4 medium-sized ramekin dishes. Mix the shrimp or prawns with the ginger, spring onions, sesame oil and soy sauce. Season with salt and divide the mixture between the 4 ramekins. Put the ramekins in a steamer.

Crack the eggs into a bowl and weigh them to work out how much stock you need. Lightly beat the eggs to break them up, but without letting them get foamy. Add the stock – it needs to be 3 times the amount of egg by weight – then add the soy sauce, mirin and garlic. Stir the stock mixture into the eggs, again making sure you don't work too much air into them, then strain into a jug. Season, then carefully pour the custard into the 4 ramekins.

Set the steamer over a pan of barely simmering water and partially cover it with a lid. Simmer for about 20 minutes until the custards are just set – they should still have a little wobble to them. Carefully remove the ramekins from the steamer and place them on serving plates. Garnish the custards with coriander and serve with asparagus.

Teriyaki chicken salad

Serves 4

6 chicken drumsticks
2 tbsp sunflower or groundnut oil
2 tsp sesame oil

Teriyaki sauce
50ml dark soy sauce
100ml mirin
1 tbsp rice wine vinegar
	or cider vinegar
1 tbsp light brown soft sugar
15g root ginger, sliced
3 fat garlic cloves, sliced
black pepper (optional)

Ranch dressing
50g soured cream
50g buttermilk
30g mayonnaise
1 tbsp rice wine or cider vinegar
pinch of sugar
1 tsp garlic powder
dash of Worcestershire sauce
dash of hot sauce (such as
	Tabasco)
salt and black pepper

Salad
1 large iceberg lettuce, shredded
200g radishes, sliced
200g cherry tomatoes, halved
6 spring onions, sliced (whites
	and greens separated)
a few coriander sprigs, chopped,
	to garnish
2 tsp sesame seeds, to garnish

This is one of our favourite salads – rich, comforting and packed with flavour. It really is worth steaming the chicken drumsticks as we suggest below, as you get a much better texture on the skin that way. And you can use the steaming liquid as a light stock in another recipe.

First cook the drumsticks. Put them in a steamer basket and steam over simmering water until cooked through, which should take about 20 minutes. The skin will shrink and become much less flabby during this process.

To make the teriyaki sauce, whisk everything together. Do not add salt – the soy sauce will reduce when cooked and become saltier as it does so. Add some black pepper if you like.

To make the ranch dressing, whisk everything together and season with salt and pepper. Taste and adjust the amount of vinegar, sugar and hot sauce to your liking.

As soon as the chicken is cool enough to handle, cut or pull the meat away from the bones, discarding any tendons or cartilage as you go.

Heat the sunflower or groundnut oil in a wok. When you can see the air above the oil shimmer, add the chicken and stir-fry until well browned. Pour in the teriyaki sauce and continue to stir regularly until it has reduced into a sticky sauce around the chicken. Drizzle over the sesame oil.

Put the lettuce, radishes, tomatoes and the whites of the spring onions into a salad bowl and pour over the ranch dressing. Toss to coat everything, then add the chicken. Garnish with the coriander, spring onion greens and sesame seeds before serving.

Potato salad with ham

Serves 4

1 small onion, finely sliced
1½ tbsp cider vinegar
500g salad potatoes, halved
     if large
100g peas, blanched for 1 minute
150g ham hock, roughly torn
100g watercress or other salad
     greens
leaves from a few mint sprigs
salt and black pepper

Dressing
4 tbsp olive oil
2 tsp wholegrain mustard
1 tsp honey
½ tsp dried mint

A potato salad in its many forms is always a go-to comfort dish and we think this recipe is one of the best. If you make the ham hock and lentil soup on page 26 – which we thoroughly recommend – this is a great way to use up the ham. We like to dress the salad with a mustardy vinaigrette rather than mayonnaise and the trick is to add the dressing to the potatoes while they're still warm.

First put the onion slices in a small bowl and sprinkle them with salt. Add the vinegar and leave the onion to stand for half an hour.

Cook the salad potatoes in plenty of boiling water until tender, then drain. Blanch the green beans in boiling water for 3 minutes, then drain and refresh under cold water.

Make the dressing. Strain the onions and put the liquid into a bowl. Add the remaining dressing ingredients to the bowl and whisk together. Taste and add salt if necessary and plenty of black pepper.

Pour most of the dressing over the potatoes while they are still warm and leave them to cool to room temperature.

To assemble, put the potatoes, peas, ham hock, watercress and mint leaves in a large salad bowl. Pour over the remaining salad dressing and toss to combine. Serve immediately.

Sloppy joes

Serves 4

2 tbsp olive oil
1 onion, finely chopped
1 green pepper, finely chopped
400g beef mince
1 tsp dried oregano
1 tsp garlic powder
2 tsp mustard powder
1 tsp hot paprika
1 tbsp dark brown soft sugar
400g can of chopped tomatoes
a few drops of liquid smoke
    (optional)
salt and black pepper

To serve
1 small onion, thinly sliced
2 tbsp cider vinegar
¼ tsp chilli flakes (optional)
100g Cheddar cheese, grated
4 large baps or burger buns
pickled jalapeños (optional)

No, this is not your first kiss, but a nice messy feast! There are lots of stories about who first came up with the idea for this American goody, but whoever did, we have to thank them. Tasty at any time of day, this even makes a nice breakfast dish over muffins or waffles instead of in a bun. Use a wide pan if you can, as this will allow the mixture to reduce more quickly.

Before you start making the meat mixture, prepare the onion for serving. Put the onion in a small bowl with half a teaspoon of salt and add the vinegar and chilli flakes, if using. Leave to stand for half an hour.

Heat the oil in a lidded sauté pan or a wide saucepan. Add the onion and green pepper and sauté over a medium-high heat until both have softened and taken on some colour. Turn up the heat and add the beef mince, then stir-fry until the meat is well browned.

Sprinkle in all the seasonings and the sugar, then add salt and pepper. Stir for another minute, then pour in the tomatoes. Rinse out the can with 100ml of water and add this too. Cover the pan with a lid, then bring to the boil and cook for 5 minutes. Remove the lid and continue to simmer until the mixture is well reduced. The mixture needs to be very thick so it can be spooned into a bun without excess liquid making the bun collapse.

Add liquid smoke if using, just a few drops at a time, stirring well between each addition and tasting to make sure you don't overdo it. If you don't have any liquid smoke, you could season with smoked salt instead of regular.

Preheat the grill to a medium heat. Divide the cheese between the 4 tops of the buns and put them under the grill to help melt the cheese. Pile the meat sauce on to the base of the buns. Add onions and jalapeños, if using, then add the cheesy tops. Serve immediately.

Bratwursts in beer

Serves 4

1 tbsp olive or sunflower oil
8 bratwurst sausages
25g butter
3 large onions, sliced
leaves from a thyme sprig
pinch of caraway seeds (optional)
1 tbsp demerara sugar
250ml beer (we used a mild
    Weissbier)
150ml chicken stock
salt and black pepper

To serve
300g sauerkraut (about half
    a large jar)
large hot dog buns
ketchup, mustard or condiments
    of your choice

My wife's birthday falls between Christmas and New Year and I decided to put on a German Christmas market party to celebrate. I put out a tray of bratwurst and onions, a pile of buns and a big bowl of sauerkraut, provided plenty of ketchup and mustard, then let everyone help themselves. I fed thirty people quite easily and they all loved it – a nice change from Christmas food. You can use any kind of sausages you like and there's a huge range of German sausages available online. This recipe is for four, but you can scale it up and add more sausages with the same amount of liquid. (Dave)

Heat the oil in a large sauté pan. Add the bratwursts and brown them thoroughly on all sides. Remove them from the pan and set aside.

Melt the butter in the pan and add the onions and thyme. Fry over a medium-high heat until the onions have coloured and crisped around the edges. Add the caraway seeds, if using, and sprinkle over the sugar. Stir until the sugar has dissolved around the onions, then pour in the beer and chicken stock. Season with salt and pepper and put the bratwursts back in the pan.

Bring to the boil, then partially cover the pan with a lid. Turn the heat down and leave to simmer until the bratwursts are cooked through. This should take about 20 minutes.

Taste the sauerkraut. If you find it too salty or acidic, rinse it gently, then put it in a saucepan with a splash of water to heat through.

Serve the bratwursts in buns with the onions, sauerkraut and plenty of your favourite condiments.

Stuffed peppers

Serves 4

4 large bell peppers
    (or 6 medium/8 small)

Filling
2 tbsp olive oil
1 onion, finely chopped
400g lamb mince
3 garlic cloves, finely chopped
1 tsp ground cumin
½ tsp ground cinnamon
½ tsp ground ginger
200g canned chopped tomatoes
50g basmati rice, well rinsed and
    soaked for 15 minutes
75ml chicken stock or water
small bunch of dill, finely chopped
½ tsp dried mint
zest of 1 lemon

Yoghurt & dill sauce
2 tbsp olive oil
15g butter
2 large onions, finely sliced
generous pinch of sugar
300g plain yoghurt
small bunch of dill, finely chopped
½ tsp dried mint

To serve
green salad

Bell peppers make ideal containers for a delicious stuffing and these are perfect for a light meal or to pop into your lunch box. The stuffing is beautifully spiced and these go down a treat with the yoghurt and dill sauce.

Preheat the oven to 200°C/Fan 180°C/Gas 6. Cut the top off each pepper, then remove the seeds and any thick white membrane. Place the peppers upside down in a roasting tin, add the caps too and drizzle with olive oil. Bake for 20 minutes to start the softening process.

To make the filling, heat the oil in a saucepan. Add the onion and sauté over a medium heat until lightly browned around the edges and turning translucent. Turn the heat up to high and add the mince. Break it up with a wooden spoon and leave it to brown on the underside, then stir and repeat until it is well browned. Add the garlic and continue to cook for a couple of minutes.

Stir in the spices, followed by the tomatoes, drained rice and the stock or water. Season with salt and pepper, then bring to the boil. Turn down the heat, cover the pan and cook until the rice is done – this will take about 15 minutes. Remove the lid and leave the filling to simmer, uncovered, until the liquid has reduced. Stir in all but a tablespoon of the dill , the dried mint and all the lemon zest.

Divide the filling between the peppers, then place them back in the roasting tin. Roast for a further 30 minutes until the peppers are completely cooked through. Sprinkle with the remaining dill.

For the yoghurt sauce, heat the olive oil and butter in a frying pan. Add the onions with a generous pinch of sugar and fry quite briskly over a medium heat until well browned. Season them with salt and pepper, then drain on kitchen paper. Finely chop half the onions and stir them through the yoghurt along with the dill and mint. Season well and garnish with the remaining onions. Serve the peppers with the sauce on the side and some green salad.

easy
comforts

Vegetable & white bean bake

Serves 4

500g cauliflower, cut into small
    florets
250g broccoli, cut into small
    florets
1 tbsp olive oil
1 onion, finely chopped
2 garlic cloves, finely chopped
400g spinach, chopped
50g rocket, chopped
2 x 400g cans of cannellini beans,
    drained
zest of 1 lemon
150g cream cheese
150g crème fraiche
150g cherry tomatoes
a few basil leaves
150g soft goat's cheese, thinly
    sliced
75g hard goat's cheese (such as
    goat's milk Gouda), grated
salt and black pepper

Packed with lovely veg and easy to make, this is a really good comforting supper. The crème fraiche and cream cheese combine to make a sauce that coats the vegetables and beans and soothes all your cares away. A great midweek meal.

Preheat the oven to 200°C/Fan 180°C/Gas 6.

Put a splash of water in the base of a large saucepan. Add the cauliflower, then place the broccoli on top. Put a lid on the pan and leave the vegetables to steam for about 5 minutes until they are tender to the point of a knife.

Heat the oil in a large, flameproof casserole dish – one about 28cm in diameter is ideal. Sauté the onion until soft and translucent, then add the garlic and cook for a further 2 minutes. Add the spinach and rocket to the casserole dish and cook until they have completely wilted down. Stir in the beans and lemon zest, then season with salt and pepper.

Whisk the cream cheese and crème fraiche together and thin the mixture with 75ml of water. Pour this over the contents of the casserole dish and stir to combine. Add the cauliflower and broccoli, pushing them down into the sauce, then add the cherry tomatoes and basil leaves, spacing them out evenly.

Arrange the slices of soft goat's cheese over the top, then sprinkle over the grated hard cheese. Bake in the oven for about half an hour until the top is browned and the sauce is bubbling through.

Soba noodles with miso mushrooms

Serves 4

Sauce

75g miso paste
2 tsp honey
3 tbsp dark soy sauce
1 tbsp rice vinegar
1 tbsp mirin
salt and black pepper

Noodles

400g soba noodles
2 tsp sesame oil
1 tbsp soy sauce

Mushrooms

1 tbsp vegetable oil
500g mushrooms, sliced
25g root ginger, cut into
    matchsticks
3 garlic cloves, finely chopped

To finish

1 tbsp sesame oil
sesame seeds
4 spring onions, sliced
a few coriander sprigs (optional)

Use any mushrooms you like but we favour a mixture of shiitake and chestnut. You could add a little asparagus too if you fancy. This is a nice simple, tasty noodle dish for a speedy supper that'll leave you feeling happy and satisfied.

First make the sauce. Whisk everything together and taste for seasoning. Add a little salt and pepper if necessary.

Cook the noodles according to the packet instructions. Make sure you cook them in plenty of water and start testing for doneness after 2–3 minutes as they can overcook very quickly. Drain the noodles thoroughly and run them under cold water to stop them cooking. Toss them in the sesame oil and soy sauce and set aside.

For the mushrooms, heat the vegetable oil in a wok. When the air over the oil is shimmering, add the mushrooms and stir-fry briskly for a few minutes until just cooked. Add the ginger and garlic and cook for a further couple of minutes, then pour in the sauce. Bring to the boil and simmer for 2 minutes.

Add the noodles to the wok and toss them gently to warm them through. Divide everything between 4 bowls and garnish with a little more sesame oil, sesame seeds, spring onions and coriander.

Risotto carbonara

Serves 4

1 tbsp olive oil
150g pancetta lardons
30g butter
1 onion, finely chopped
3 garlic cloves, finely chopped
leaves from a large thyme sprig
300g risotto rice
100ml white wine
1 litre chicken stock, warmed
2 egg yolks
50g Parmesan, grated
salt and black pepper

What are the most comforting dishes you can think of? We bet risotto and spaghetti carbonara are going to be high on the list, so you're going to love our genius idea of combining the two to make a dish that's like a big comfy hug. Apologies to Italian purists but we love this.

Heat the olive oil in a large sauté pan and add the pancetta lardons. Fry them over a high heat until crisp and browned, then remove them with a slotted spoon and set aside.

Add half the butter to the pan. When it has melted, add the onion and sauté it over a low-medium heat until soft and translucent. Add the garlic, thyme and rice, then stir until the rice is glossy with oil and butter. Season with salt and black pepper.

Pour in the wine and bring to the boil. When the wine has almost completely boiled off, add a ladleful of stock. Stir the stock into the rice over a medium heat and keep stirring until most of it has been absorbed by the rice. Repeat until you have used all the stock – this process will take at least 20 minutes. By this time the rice should be slightly al dente and surrounded by a creamy sauce. Have a taste – the rice should still have a very little bite to it.

Beat in the egg yolks, followed by the rest of the butter and half the Parmesan. Stir in two-thirds of the pancetta, and leave the risotto to stand for a couple of minutes to heat through.

Serve garnished with the rest of the pancetta and grated Parmesan.

Special fried rice

Serves 4

2 tbsp vegetable oil
2 eggs, beaten
200g shelled raw prawns
    (optional)
2 bacon rashers, finely diced
1 onion, diced
1 red pepper, diced
1 carrot, finely sliced on the
    diagonal
100g baby corn, sliced into rounds
10g root ginger, cut into
    matchsticks
2 garlic cloves, finely chopped
½ tsp Chinese 5-spice powder
150g cooked chicken, shredded
150g peas, defrosted if frozen
400g cooked basmati rice, chilled
4 spring onions, finely sliced
    (include the greens)
1 tsp sesame oil
salt and black pepper

Sauce
2 tbsp soy sauce
1 tbsp rice vinegar
1 tbsp rice wine
1 tsp hot sauce (optional)

To serve
soy sauce
chilli oil

Fried rice is a popular comfort dish in many parts of Asia. Quick and easy to make, it's the perfect supper when you've got some bits and bobs in the fridge that need using up – and it's dead good too! We've listed everything but the kitchen sink here but feel free to use whatever you fancy. Adding raw prawns makes the dish a bit special and brings extra flavour, but if you prefer, you could add some cooked ones at the end instead.

Mix together the sauce ingredients in a small bowl.

Heat 2 teaspoons of the vegetable oil in a wok. Season the eggs with a pinch of salt and add them to the wok. Scramble very quickly, then as soon as the eggs are set, turn them out on to a plate.

Wipe out the wok and add the remaining oil. Add the prawns, if using, and stir-fry them until pink and cooked through. Remove them from the wok and set aside. Add the bacon and fry until crisp, then add the onion, red pepper, carrot and baby corn. Stir-fry over a high heat until just al dente, then add the ginger and garlic. Sprinkle in the Chinese 5-spice powder and continue to stir-fry for 2 minutes.

Add the chicken and peas to the wok and fry for one minute, then add the rice. Continue to stir-fry until the rice is heated through, then pour the sauce over the contents of the wok. Stir-fry for another minute, then stir through the prawns, if using, the spring onions and the scrambled eggs. Leave to stand over the heat for a couple of minutes.

Drizzle over the sesame oil and serve immediately, with soy sauce and chilli oil at the table for everyone to add.

Creamy lemon pasta

Serves 4

500g linguine
6 garlic cloves, left unpeeled
1 large thyme sprig
10g butter
zest of 2 lemons
150g Pecorino or Parmesan
    cheese, grated
squeeze of lemon juice
salt and black pepper

To serve
chilli flakes
lemon wedges

Everyone loves a pasta supper and this recipe is simple and very comforting. Just imagine yourself enjoying it on a terrace overlooking the Amalfi coast and it'll taste even better. It's nice as it is or you could add some chicken or roast veg if you like. Do follow our method below, as we find it prevents the pasta clumping together.

Bring a large pan of water to the boil and add plenty of salt. Add the linguine, garlic cloves and thyme, then cook until the linguine is just al dente.

Ladle about 500ml of the cooking liquid out into a jug and set it aside, then drain the pasta. Tip the pasta back into the pan and remove the garlic cloves and thyme. Squeeze out the garlic flesh and put it in a bowl that's large enough to hold all the pasta later. Add the butter and lemon zest to the pasta and keep it warm.

Add 100g of the cheese to the garlic paste in the bowl and gradually add the 500ml of cooking liquid. It will initially form a paste – keep adding liquid until you have a creamy sauce the consistency of single cream. Add the pasta to the bowl and stir until all the strands of pasta are coated in the sauce.

Serve the pasta in shallow bowls and sprinkle over the rest of the grated cheese. Serve with chilli flakes and wedges of lemon to add at the table.

Sausage pasta

Serves 4

1 tbsp olive oil
1 large onion, finely chopped
6 sausages, skinned
2 garlic cloves, finely chopped
1 tsp dried sage
100ml white wine
300ml chicken or vegetable
    stock or water
200g pumpkin or butternut
    squash, cut into 1cm dice
200g kale, chopped
400g short pasta
75g cream cheese
salt and black pepper

To serve
grated Parmesan

We always seem to get good feedback about our sausage recipes. A great family supper, this is a hearty and nourishing dish with an autumnal vibe and it's a clever way to sneak some vegetables into the kids. If you don't fancy kale, use peas or another green veg and choose whatever type of sausages you prefer – we like garlicky ones. The cream cheese works well, as it has a good flavour and doesn't split like cream tends to do.

Heat the olive oil in a large flameproof casserole dish. Add the onion and sauté until soft and translucent.

Turn up the heat and add the sausage meat. Break it up with the back of a spoon and cook until seared on all sides. Stir in the garlic and sage, cook for a further minute, then pour in the wine. Bring to the boil, stirring constantly to deglaze the pan, then pour in the stock or water.

Add the butternut squash and kale to the pan, pushing the kale down as much as possible. Season with salt and pepper. Bring to the boil, then cover the pan and simmer until the butternut squash and kale are both tender.

Meanwhile, cook the pasta in plenty of salted, boiling water until al dente. Drain it into a colander.

Stir the cream cheese into the sausage mixture. You'll find that the butternut squash will start breaking up and this will help give the sauce a sweet, creamy finish. Add the pasta to the sauce and stir until well combined. Season with plenty of black pepper and serve with grated Parmesan.

Nduja linguine

Serves 4

500g linguine

Sauce
2 tbsp olive oil
1 small onion, very finely chopped
3 garlic cloves, very finely
    chopped
250g cherry tomatoes, puréed
1 tsp dried oregano
150g nduja
50ml vodka
50ml double cream
salt and black pepper

To serve
basil leaves
grated Parmesan
chilli flakes (optional)

Nduja – that spicy pork and pepper paste from Italy – has become a great favourite of ours and we think it works brilliantly in this quick pasta recipe. It does vary in heat, so if you like things hot, hot, hot, maybe add a few chilli flakes to the mix. You might be surprised to see vodka in the ingredients list, but it really does help to bring all the flavours together and gives extra oomph to the dish. Be sure to let the vodka cook for long enough though, so your supper doesn't taste boozy.

First make the sauce. Heat the oil in a saucepan, add the onion and cook over a low-medium heat until soft and translucent. Add the garlic and continue to cook for another 2–3 minutes.

Pour in the cherry tomatoes and add the oregano and nduja. Break up the nduja as much as possible, so it crumbles and starts to dissolve into the tomatoes. Season with plenty of salt and pepper. Bring the sauce to the boil, then turn down the heat and leave to simmer while you cook the pasta.

Cook the linguine in plenty of salted, boiling water until al dente. Drain the pasta, reserving a ladleful of the cooking water, then tip the pasta back into the saucepan.

Add the vodka to the sauce and let it simmer for a couple of minutes before adding the double cream and about 100ml of the cooking water. Simmer for a few more minutes – the cooking liquid will help thicken the sauce.

Pour the sauce over the linguine and mix thoroughly. Serve in shallow pasta bowls and garnish with basil leaves and grated Parmesan. Serve with a bowl of chilli flakes for anyone who wants some extra heat.

Filipino noodles

Serves 4

2 tbsp groundnut or sunflower oil
1 red onion, diced
300g pork escalopes, thinly sliced
2 carrots, cut into slim batons
1 red pepper, thinly sliced
100g green beans, trimmed
200g cabbage, shredded
3 garlic cloves, finely chopped
200ml chicken stock
2 tbsp light soy sauce
1 tbsp dark soy sauce
2 tsp sriracha (optional)
juice of 1 lime
juice of ½ clementine or
    mandarin (optional)
salt and black pepper

Noodles
250g rice vermicelli, cooked
    according to the packet
    instructions
1 tsp sesame oil
1 tbsp soy sauce

To serve
2 spring onions, finely sliced

A wonderful Filipino nurse named Guia looked after me during my time in hospital. One day when I was having chemo, she brought me in her favourite noodle dish, called pancit. It's hard to eat much when you're having treatment but I inhaled this – it was so good – and so did my wife who was sitting beside me. It gave me great comfort and I couldn't wait to cook it myself. Traditionally, this is garnished with calamansi lime juice which is difficult to get in the UK but a good substitute is ordinary lime with a squeeze of clementine or mandarin. (Dave)

Heat the oil in a large wok or sauté pan. Add the onion and stir-fry over a high heat until it's starting to take on some colour. Add the pork and continue to stir-fry until well browned. Add the remaining vegetables and stir-fry for 5 minutes until they start to reduce in volume, then add the garlic and cook for another minute.

Whisk the chicken stock, soy sauces and sriracha, if using, and pour the mixture over the contents of the pan. Cover and leave to braise for a few minutes until the vegetables are just cooked through but still have a little bite to them, then remove the lid and allow the liquid to reduce.

Start the noodles while you are simmering the pork and vegetables. They will probably need a few minutes of soaking but check the packet instructions. When they are soft, drain them thoroughly and cool quickly under cold water. Dress them with the sesame oil and soy sauce.

Add the noodles to the pan and toss to combine with the pork and vegetables. Mix the lime and clementine juices together, if using both, then pour over the noodles. Taste and season with pepper if necessary, then serve immediately.

Chicken stroganoff

Serves 4

2 boneless, skinless chicken
    breasts
2 tbsp olive oil
15g butter
1 large onion, finely chopped
250g white mushrooms, sliced
2 garlic cloves, finely chopped
100ml vermouth or white wine
1 tbsp Dijon mustard
2 tsp hot paprika
leaves from a large thyme sprig,
    chopped
150ml chicken stock
100ml soured cream
squeeze of lemon juice
2 tbsp finely chopped parsley,
    to garnish
salt and black pepper

To serve
rice, wide noodles or potatoes

The classic stroganoff is made with beef but our chicken version is just as tasty and makes a super-quick supper that will fill your tum and warm your heart. Be sure to prep the chicken as we suggest below, as it helps it stay nice and tender. Serve with rice, noodles or potatoes – or even chips!

First, cut the chicken breasts in half. The easiest way to do this is to lay the breast flat, hold it in place with one hand, then cut through from the side. You will end up with 2 flat pieces. Finely slice each piece, then season with salt and black pepper.

Heat a tablespoon of the oil in a large sauté pan with a lid and quickly fry the chicken until lightly browned. Remove it from the pan and set aside.

Add the remaining olive oil and the butter to the pan. When the butter has melted, add the onion and cook it over a medium-low heat until soft and translucent. Turn up the heat slightly and add the mushrooms. Cook for several minutes, then add the garlic and cook for a couple more minutes.

Pour over the vermouth or white wine and allow at least half of it to boil off, then stir in the mustard, paprika and thyme. Pour in the chicken stock and season with salt and pepper.

Put the chicken back in the pan, then bring to the boil and cover. Simmer for 5 minutes, then stir in the soured cream. Continue to simmer until piping hot again, then taste for seasoning and add a squeeze of lemon juice. Garnish with a little finely chopped parsley and serve with your choice of side dish.

Chicken tray bake

Serves 4

500g waxy potatoes, thickly
    sliced
4 tbsp olive oil
1 fennel, cut into wedges
4 chicken thighs, on the bone
1 tsp dried oregano
100ml white wine
150ml chicken stock
1 tbsp white wine vinegar
leaves from 3 tarragon sprigs,
    finely chopped, plus more
    to garnish
2 garlic cloves, grated or crushed
1 lemon, cut in half lengthways
    and thinly sliced
2 courgettes, cut into slices,
    diagonally
200g asparagus spears, trimmed
8 baby leeks, trimmed
leaves from a few parsley sprigs,
    finely chopped
salt and black pepper

We've come up with quite a few chicken tray bakes in our time but we are extra happy with this one. Everything works together to make a great one-pot supper. We add the ingredients in three stages so nothing ends up overcooked – it's really no trouble to do this and it does make a big difference to the result. It's best to get chicken thighs on the bone, as they cook better in a tray bake and are cheaper too.

Preheat the oven to 200°C/Fan 180°C/Gas 6. Bring a pan of water to the boil, add salt, then the potato slices and cook for 5 minutes. Drain the potatoes thoroughly, then tip them back into the saucepan and leave over a low heat to steam briefly so they are as dry as possible.

Put a tablespoon of the oil into a large bowl. Add the fennel and potatoes and toss until they are well coated. Season them with salt and arrange them on a large roasting tin. Put a little more oil into the same bowl, add the chicken thighs and make sure they are well covered in the oil. Sprinkle them with salt, pepper and the oregano, then place them on top of the fennel and potatoes.

Place the tin in the oven and roast for 20 minutes. Whisk the wine, stock and vinegar together and add the chopped tarragon and garlic, then pour this mixture around the chicken, potatoes and fennel. Put the remaining oil into a bowl and add the lemon slices, courgettes, asparagus and leeks.

Add the lemon and courgettes to the tin and roast for another 15 minutes. Then add the asparagus and leeks and roast for a final 10 minutes. Everything should be just tender and the chicken should be well browned. Mix the parsley and extra tarragon together and sprinkle over the tray bake before serving.

Baked potatoes with devilled black pudding

Serves 4

4 large baking potatoes
1 tbsp olive oil
butter
salt

Filling
2 tbsp olive oil
400g black pudding, cut into
    rounds
1 large onion, diced
2 garlic cloves, finely chopped
50ml dry sherry or white wine
200ml chicken stock
1 tbsp tomato purée
2 tsp Dijon mustard
1 tsp smoked paprika
½ tsp hot paprika or cayenne
dash of Worcestershire sauce
1 tbsp soured cream
squeeze of lemon juice
small bunch of parsley, finely
    chopped

Baked potatoes are an all-time favourite in the comfort food stakes and with this black pudding filling they make a supper to be proud of. Just handle the black pudding carefully so it doesn't break up too much. A good Friday night feast.

First cook the potatoes. Preheat the oven to 200°C/Fan 180°C/Gas 6. Pierce the potatoes all over with a skewer, then rub them with olive oil and sprinkle with salt. Put them on a baking tray in the oven and bake for 1–1½ hours, depending on size. Alternatively, cook the potatoes in an air fryer or a microwave if you prefer.

To make the filling, heat a tablespoon of the oil in a frying pan. Add the black pudding and sear until it's just cooked through and both sides are crisp and blackened. Remove it from the frying pan and set aside.

Add the remaining tablespoon of olive oil to the pan followed by the onion. Sauté over a medium heat until softened and lightly browned, then add the garlic. Stir for another minute, add the sherry and bring to the boil. Allow most of the sherry to boil off, then pour in the stock. Stir in the tomato purée, mustard, spices and Worcestershire sauce, then season with salt and pepper.

Simmer for several minutes until the sauce has reduced to the consistency of pouring cream, then stir in the soured cream. Taste and add a squeeze of lemon juice.

Carefully dice the rounds of black pudding – you don't want them to crumble too much – and put them in the pan of sauce to heat through. Try not to stir the black pudding at this stage as it will break up if you do. When it is piping hot, sprinkle with the chopped parsley.

Cut open the potatoes. Season them with salt and add a generous knob of butter. Divide the sauce between the potatoes and serve immediately.

Bacon chops with parsley sauce

Serves 4

1 tbsp olive or sunflower oil
4 bacon chops
1 tbsp cider vinegar

Parsley sauce
400ml milk
2 bay leaves
slice of onion
2 cloves
a few peppercorns
25g butter
25g flour
½ tsp English mustard powder
  (optional)
25g curly parsley, very finely
  chopped
salt and black pepper

Bacon chops are a nice change from your regular pork chops and are worth looking out for. They are basically back bacon cut thickly instead of into rashers and can be smoked or unsmoked. The chops are perfect with parsley sauce and a dollop of mustard but if you can't find any, you can make this dish with gammon steaks instead.

First make the sauce. Pour the milk into a saucepan and add the bay leaves, onion, cloves and peppercorns. Slowly heat until the milk is almost at the boil, then remove the pan from the heat and set aside. Leave to infuse until the milk is tepid, then strain into a jug.

Heat the butter in a saucepan. When it has melted, stir in the flour and the mustard powder, if using, to make a roux. Gradually add the milk, a little at a time to start with, making sure the roux is completely lump free before the next addition. Continue adding the milk until it is all incorporated and the sauce has the consistency of thick pouring cream. Simmer the sauce for a few minutes, stirring regularly to prevent it from catching, then stir in the parsley and taste for seasoning. Add salt and pepper as necessary, then cover and keep the sauce warm.

To cook the chops, heat the oil in a large frying pan. When it's hot, add the chops and cook them for 4 or 5 minutes on each side until well browned. Remove them from the pan and set aside to keep warm.

Mix the cider vinegar with 50ml of water and add this to the frying pan. Stir vigorously, letting the liquid bubble up, until you have a small amount of rich brown jus. Drizzle this over the bacon chops, then serve them with the parsley sauce and some green vegetables.

Arroz al horno

Serves 4

2 tbsp olive oil
150g black pudding, sliced
100g hot cooking chorizo, sliced
2 red onions, sliced into slim
    wedges
2 red peppers, diced
3 garlic cloves, finely chopped
100g tomatoes, fresh or tinned,
    finely chopped or puréed
1 tbsp smoked paprika
pinch of saffron, soaked in 2 tbsp
    warm water (optional)
2 bay leaves
leaves from a few rosemary sprigs,
    finely chopped
zest and juice of 1 lemon
1 litre chicken stock
400g can of chickpeas
300g paella rice
1 head of garlic
chopped parsley, to garnish
salt and black pepper

During one of my stays in hospital I asked my Spanish nurse, Monica, what her favourite comfy dish was and she came back with this – arroz al horno, which means 'rice in the oven'. Filling and warming, this is a much-loved Spanish classic and here's our version. Hope you like it, Monica, and thanks for the idea. Traditionally, this would be made with morcilla but we're happy with British black pudding which is firmer and easier to fry. (Dave)

Preheat the oven to 200°C/Fan 180°C/Gas 6.

Heat a tablespoon of the olive oil in a wide, shallow, flameproof casserole dish. Quickly fry the black pudding, then remove it with a slotted spoon and set it aside. Add the chorizo and fry until lightly browned, then remove it from the pan and set it aside with the black pudding.

Heat the remaining oil in the casserole dish and add the onions and peppers. Sauté until they have softened and the onion is translucent, then stir in the garlic. Cook for another minute, then add the tomatoes, paprika, the saffron and its soaking water, if using, the herbs and the lemon zest. Stir for a minute, then pour in the stock and add the chickpeas. Season with plenty of salt and pepper. Bring to the boil and cook for a couple of minutes.

Put the black pudding and chorizo back in the casserole dish. Sprinkle in the rice as evenly as you can, pushing it under the liquid where necessary but without stirring. Season again.

Pierce the head of garlic all over with the tip of a sharp knife, making sure you go right through each clove. Push the garlic into the centre of the casserole dish so only the top is left exposed.

Put the dish in the oven and bake, uncovered, for 20–25 minutes until the rice has absorbed the liquid and is swollen and tender. Remove the dish from the oven, cover with a tea towel and a lid, and leave to stand for 10 minutes. This step isn't essential, but it does improve the texture of the rice.

Pour over the lemon juice and serve sprinkled with parsley. Break open the head of garlic and divide the cloves between each serving – the garlic flesh can be squeezed out and eaten with the rice.

Sausage tray bake

Serves 4

8 large sausages
3 red onions, cut into wedges
2 tbsp olive oil
cloves from a head of garlic,
    separated and unpeeled
300g sprouting broccoli
1 tsp wholegrain Dijon mustard
100ml white wine
250g cooked lentils – puy, brown
    or green (100g uncooked, or
    the equivalent of 1 can
    or pouch)
a few rosemary sprigs
300g cherry tomatoes
leaves from a few parsley sprigs,
    finely chopped
salt and black pepper

This one's a belter – simple, straightforward and tasty. You can never have too many tray bakes – or too many sausage suppers for that matter – so give this recipe a try. We think you'll enjoy it. It's hearty and warming but contains plenty of vegetables too, so is good for your five a day.

Preheat the oven to 200°C/Fan 180°C/Gas 6.

Put the sausages and onions in a large roasting tin and pour over the olive oil. Give the tin a shake to coat everything in oil. Add the garlic cloves, keeping them together for easy removal. Roast in the oven for 25 minutes.

Bring a kettleful of water to the boil. Put the sprouting broccoli in a bowl and pour the boiling water over it. Leave to stand for a minute, then drain.

Remove the garlic cloves from the roasting tin and squish the flesh out of them. Put the flesh in a bowl with the mustard and white wine and whisk together with 100ml of water. Add the lentils and mix thoroughly.

Add the lentil mixture to the roasting tin, then shake the tin well to distribute the lentils evenly around the sausages and red onions. Season with salt and pepper. Sprinkle over the rosemary sprigs, then arrange the sprouting broccoli over the top and season again. Roast in the oven for 15 minutes, then add the cherry tomatoes and roast for another 5 minutes.

Remove the tray bake from the oven and garnish with chopped parsley. Serve immediately.

Sausage & cabbage casserole

Serves 4

3 tbsp olive oil
8–12 sausages
1 large onion, diced
500g small waxy potatoes
large thyme sprig
1 tsp dried sage
300ml cider
200ml chicken stock
1 tbsp Dijon mustard
1 small cabbage, cut into 8 wedges
2 crisp eating apples, cored and
    cut into wedges
15g butter
salt and black pepper

Every sausage casserole we've done so far has been a hit and here's another one to enter our charts. Sausages, cabbage, apples, cider and mustard work really well together so we've combined them all in this easy recipe. A welcome feast on an autumn evening but light enough for summer too.

Heat a tablespoon of the oil in a large flameproof casserole dish and add the sausages. Fry them over a high heat until well browned on all sides, then set them aside on a plate.

Add the onion and sauté it over a medium-high heat until translucent. Add the potatoes and stir until they're well coated with the onion- and sausage-flavoured oil, then add the thyme and sage. Season with salt and pepper.

Turn up the heat and pour in the cider, then stir thoroughly to deglaze the casserole dish and make sure no brown bits are sticking to the bottom. Whisk the chicken stock with the mustard, then add this and the sausages to the dish. Bring to the boil, partially cover the dish with a lid, then turn the heat down and leave to simmer for 20 minutes.

While the sausages and potatoes are cooking, prepare the cabbage and apples. Add a tablespoon of the remaining olive oil to a large frying pan. When it's hot, add the cabbage wedges and sear them on both sides. Remove from the frying pan and set aside, then add the remaining oil and the butter. When the butter has foamed, add the apple wedges and sear them on both sides.

Add the cabbage to the casserole dish and continue to cook for another 15 minutes until the cabbage is tender to the point of a knife. Add the apples and cook for a further 5 minutes, then serve in shallow bowls.

Beef & baked bean hotpot

Serves 4 generously

1 tbsp olive oil
1 large onion, diced
400g beef mince
1 tsp dried oregano
1 small bunch of parsley, finely
    chopped
2 x 400g cans of baked beans
400g can of tomatoes
dash of Worcestershire sauce
200ml beef stock
600g floury potatoes, unpeeled
    and thinly sliced (about 3mm)
25g butter
100g mature Cheddar, grated
salt and black pepper

Our neighbour Millie brought us round a dish of this one night when I was just back from hospital. It was her stand-by meal when she was a student and it was just what we needed. We've worked on the recipe and we want you to enjoy it too. Thank you, Millie! (Dave)

Heat the olive oil in an flameproof casserole dish. Add the onion and sauté it over a medium heat for several minutes until it has taken on a little colour. Then turn up the heat and add the beef. Break it up with a wooden spoon and fry it briskly on all sides until well browned. Sprinkle in the oregano and all but a tablespoon of the parsley and stir. Season with salt and pepper.

Pour in the baked beans, tomatoes, Worcestershire sauce and stock. Bring to the boil, then turn the heat down and leave to simmer, uncovered, for about 30 minutes until the liquid has reduced by about a third. Preheat the oven to 200°C/Fan 180°C/Gas 6.

Cook the potatoes in plenty of boiling water for about 5 minutes until they are just the firm side of knife tender, then drain them and rinse under cold water. Layer the potato slices over the beef and beans, dotting butter in between each layer – you should get at least 3 layers of potato. Sprinkle over the cheese and the reserved parsley.

Bake the hotpot in the preheated oven for about 25 minutes until the cheese has melted and brown and the sauce is bubbling.

spicy
comforts

Tomato, pepper & aubergine rice

Serves 4

2 roasted red peppers (from a jar
    is fine)
200g fresh tomatoes, roughly
    chopped (or use canned)
1 scotch bonnet, deseeded
3 tbsp groundnut or sunflower oil
2 aubergines, diced
1 large red onion, finely diced
4 garlic cloves, finely chopped
2 bay leaves
1 large thyme sprig
1 tbsp mild curry powder
2 tbsp tomato purée
300g basmati rice, well rinsed
30g butter
450ml chicken or vegetable stock
a few parsley sprigs, finely
    chopped, to garnish
salt and black pepper

If you like a risotto and you like a pilaf, you'll love this – a one-pot rice dish that's the gift that keeps on giving. It makes a great supper on its own or as a side dish with some grilled meat or chicken. We like to finish it by steaming the rice over a low heat, so you get that lovely smoky, slightly burnt crust to the rice at the bottom of the pan. If you prefer, though, just steam the rice off the heat as usual.

Put the peppers, tomatoes and scotch bonnet in a food processor and blitz them until smooth, then set aside.

Heat 2 tablespoons of the oil in a large, lidded sauté pan or saucepan. Add the aubergines and fry them briskly until lightly browned, then remove them from the pan and set aside. Add the remaining oil and sauté the onion until soft and translucent, with just a hint of browning. Add the garlic, bay leaves, thyme, curry powder and tomato purée and stir for several minutes until the tomato purée smells rich and starts to separate from the oil.

Pour in the tomato and pepper mixture. Continue to cook, stirring regularly, until the mixture is quite concentrated – it should be fairly dry at this point.

Add the rice together with the butter and stir until the butter has melted, then pour over the stock. Put the diced aubergine back in the pan, making sure it's evenly spread over the rice, and season with salt and pepper. Bring to the boil, then turn down the heat and cover the pan. Leave to simmer for about 15 minutes or until all the liquid has been absorbed by the rice and the rice is cooked.

Place a tea towel over the pan and replace the lid. Leave to steam over a very low heat for another 10–15 minutes – this will help enormously with the texture of the rice and should help the rice brown a little on the bottom. Garnish with parsley and serve immediately.

Kimchi burgers

Serves 4

500g steak mince, at room
   temperature
½ Chinese cabbage, shredded
2 spring onions, shredded
50g drained kimchi, finely
   chopped
4 slices of cheese (optional)
4 large slices of gherkin
4 burger buns, cut in half
sesame seeds
salt and black pepper

Kimchi burger sauce
2 tbsp mayonnaise
1 tsp ketchup
2 tbsp kimchi juice
1 tsp gochujang or other
   chilli paste

You can't have a book on comfort food without a burger and we've dressed up our basic version with a nice bit of Korean flavour. We think the kimchi works brilliantly with the other ingredients – fusion food at its best with loads of that fab umami, savoury flavour.

First make the burgers. Season the meat with plenty of salt and pepper, then shape it into 4 patties and set them aside.

Put the Chinese cabbage and spring onions in a colander and sprinkle with salt. Mix thoroughly and leave to stand for half an hour. Gently squeeze out the excess water, then mix with the drained kimchi.

Make the burger sauce by mixing everything together. Taste for seasoning and add salt and pepper as necessary.

Heat a griddle until it's too hot to hold your hand over. Grill the burgers on one side until they are well charred. They are ready to flip when they come away easily from the griddle. Once you've flipped them, top with the cheese, if using. Continue to cook the burgers until the cheese has started to melt. Putting something over the griddle, such as a deep, domed pan lid or an upturned wok, will hurry this along if need be.

Lightly toast the burger buns on their cut sides, then assemble the burgers with the beef patties, sauce, gherkin and the kimchi-flavoured cabbage. Sprinkle with sesame seeds and top with the other half of the burger buns.

Egg makhani curry

Serves 4

1 large onion, diced
25g root ginger, peeled
    and roughly chopped
6 garlic cloves, peeled
25g butter or ghee
1 tsp ground turmeric
1 tsp chilli powder
6 hard-boiled eggs, peeled
2 tsp garam masala
½ tsp ground fenugreek
400g can of chopped tomatoes or
    passata, puréed until smooth
400g new/salad potatoes, boiled
75g yoghurt or single cream
squeeze of lemon juice
salt and black pepper

To serve
rice
a few green chillies, sliced
small bunch of coriander, chopped

The egg version of butter chicken, this is such a favourite of ours. It's the ideal dish to have when you're feeling a bit tired and you need cheering up and comforting. You can add any vegetables, but we like new potatoes for that extra carbohydrate hug. Go for yoghurt or cream as you like, but maybe add a little extra lemon juice if you use cream. The yoghurt brings its own tanginess to the dish.

Put the onion, ginger and garlic into a food processor with a generous pinch of salt. Blitz them to make a purée and set aside.

Heat the butter or ghee in a large saucepan or a flameproof casserole dish. Add the turmeric and chilli powder, then fry for a few moments. Add the hard-boiled eggs and fry them briefly on all sides so they take on some colour from the spices and start to brown – they might blister a little in places which is fine. Remove the eggs from the pan and set them aside.

Stir in the onion purée and fry for several minutes until it has reduced and is very aromatic. Sprinkle in the garam masala and fenugreek and season with salt and pepper. Continue to fry for a couple of minutes, then add the tomatoes or passata. Rinse out the tin or jar with 100ml of water and add this to the pan.

Bring to the boil, then turn the heat down and leave to simmer for 10 minutes. Stir in the yoghurt or cream and then taste – add more garam masala or chilli powder if you like.

Put the eggs back in the pan together with the potatoes and leave over a low heat to heat through gently, but don't allow the curry to boil. Check the seasoning and add salt and pepper to taste, plus a squeeze of lemon juice.

Serve with rice and garnish with chillies and coriander.

Vegetable & lentil curry

Serves 4

1 tbsp coconut oil
12 curry leaves
1 tsp mustard seeds
1 tsp nigella seeds
1 large onion, diced
600g cauliflower, cut into florets
15g root ginger, grated
4 garlic cloves, crushed or grated
1 tbsp medium curry powder
1 tsp cayenne (optional)
2 sweet potatoes, peeled and
    diced
100g red lentils or split mung dal,
    well rinsed
500ml vegetable stock or water
200g canned tomatoes
salt and black pepper

To serve
small bunch of coriander, chopped
lemon wedges
green chillies, finely sliced
naan bread (shop-bought
    or see p.266)

Here's a nice simple veggie – and vegan – curry that's really tasty. It's substantial as it is, but you could also a add a can of chickpeas if you want extra carbs. The lentils should stay nicely thick but liquid enough to form a sauce around the vegetables. A comforting dish at any time of year.

Heat the coconut oil in a large, lidded sauté pan or a shallow flameproof casserole dish. When the oil has melted, add the curry leaves and the mustard and nigella seeds. Heat until they start to crackle and pop, then stir in the onion and cauliflower. Fry over a high heat until the vegetables start to brown, then stir in the ginger, garlic, curry powder and cayenne, if using. Stir for a couple more minutes, then add the diced sweet potatoes and stir to coat them in the spices.

Add the red lentils, then pour in the stock or water. Season with plenty of salt and pepper, then add the tomatoes. Bring to the boil, then turn down the heat, cover the pan and leave to cook until the lentils have softened and broken down and the vegetables are tender. This should take 20–25 minutes. Check regularly to make sure the curry isn't catching on the bottom of the pan and add a splash of water to loosen the mixture if necessary.

Garnish with the coriander and serve with lemon wedges and sliced green chillies for extra heat. Good with some naan bread to mop the juices.

Mussels in curry sauce

Serves 4

1.75–2kg mussels

15g butter

2 shallots, finely sliced

15g root ginger, grated

2 garlic cloves, grated or crushed

2 tsp curry powder

pinch of saffron, soaked in 1 tbsp
of warm water

250ml white wine

100ml double cream

squeeze of lime juice

small bunch of coriander or
parsley, finely chopped

salt and black pepper

To serve
French bread

Mussels are great value and this spicy dish makes a nice change from the usual moules marinière. Known in France as mouclade, this is a great winter warmer and is quick to prepare. Not all the traditional recipes contain saffron, but we think it works well and we love the hint of root ginger too.

First prepare the mussels. Pull off any beards, scrape off barnacles and make sure the mussels close when sharply tapped. Discard any that don't close. Leave the mussels in cold water until you are ready to use them.

Heat the butter in a large saucepan. Add the shallots and sauté them over a medium-high heat until lightly browned. Stir in the ginger, garlic and curry powder, then season with salt and pepper and stir for another couple of minutes. Add the saffron and the white wine and stir to deglaze the base of the pan, scraping up any sticky bits.

Add the mussels to the pan and cover with a lid. Leave the mussels to steam for 3–4 minutes, shaking the pan regularly. Check that all the mussels have opened – if they haven't, cover the pan again and leave for a further minute.

Pour in the cream and reheat the liquid without bringing it to the boil. Squeeze over some lime juice, then garnish with the coriander or parsley. Remember to discard any mussels that haven't opened before serving.

Serve with French bread for mopping up the delicious juices.

Vietnamese fish curry

Serves 4

1 tbsp coconut oil
Vietnamese curry paste
   (see p.257)
2 star anise
200ml chicken or fish stock
400ml coconut milk
6 lime leaves
1–2 tbsp fish sauce
2 medium courgettes, sliced
   (optional)
150g asparagus tips (optional)
450g white fish fillets, cut into
   chunks
200g raw shelled prawns
juice of 1 lime
salt and black pepper

To garnish
50g bean sprouts
4 spring onions, shredded
mint leaves
2 chillies, finely sliced
lime wedges

To serve
steamed rice or rice noodles

This one takes us back twenty years to our time filming in Vietnam when we fell in love with the fabulous food. We use the same curry paste for this as for the noodle soup on page 28 and once that's made this dish is so speedy to put together. We like hake but any firm white fish fillets will be fine. And if you feel like going the extra mile, you could get prawns in their shells, and use the heads and shells in the stock for extra flavour.

Heat the coconut oil in a large saucepan. Add the curry paste and fry until it smells very aromatic, then add the star anise, stock, coconut milk and lime leaves. Bring to the boil, then turn the heat down to a simmer and add a tablespoon of the fish sauce. Check the seasoning and add salt and pepper to taste. Simmer for 5 minutes.

Add the courgettes and asparagus, if using, and simmer for 5 minutes. Add the fish and prawns and continue to simmer over a very low heat until they are just cooked through. Taste and add more fish sauce if you think it necessary, followed by the lime juice.

Serve over rice or noodles and put the garnishes on the table so everyone can help themselves.

Spiced crab omelette

Serves 2

4–6 eggs
butter, for frying

Filling
1 tbsp coconut oil
½ tsp mustard seeds
1 small onion, finely chopped
10g root ginger, grated
2 garlic cloves, finely chopped
1 green chilli, finely chopped
½ tsp curry powder or garam
  masala
100g cherry tomatoes, halved
  or quartered
small bunch of coriander, finely
  chopped
100g white crab meat
squeeze of lime juice
salt and black pepper

The inspiration for this comes from Jay Fai, purveyor of the best street food in Bangkok – his crab omelettes are incredible. Crab is a real treat and this omelette has a light summery taste but is still luxurious and comforting. We've used white crab, but you could get one of those mixed pots of brown and white meat which are a bit cheaper.

First make the filling. Heat the coconut oil in a frying pan. When it's hot, add the mustard seeds and let them splutter in the oil. Add the onion and fry it over a medium heat until it's translucent. Stir in the ginger, garlic and chilli and cook for another couple of minutes. Add the curry powder or garam masala and stir for another minute.

Add the cherry tomatoes and season with salt and pepper. Cook, stirring regularly, for just 3–4 minutes – you want the tomatoes to soften but still keep their shape. Add the coriander and crab meat and stir to combine with the rest of the ingredients. Then add a squeeze of lime and set the filling aside to keep warm.

To make the omelettes, use 2 or 3 eggs per person depending on appetite. Beat 2 or 3 eggs thoroughly and season with salt and pepper. Heat an omelette pan and add a knob of butter when the pan is hot. The butter should immediately melt and foam. Pour in the eggs and swirl them around in the pan – they should start setting straight away. Pull the set egg in from the edges of the pan to the centre, allowing uncooked egg to run into the space left and set. Keep doing this until the eggs are almost completely set.

Put half the crab mixture down the centre of the omelette. Fold over the sides and roll the omelette out of the pan on to a plate. Repeat with the remaining eggs and crab mixture, then serve at once.

Chipotle prawn tacos

Serves 4

Prawns
zest and juice of 1 lime
1 tbsp olive oil
2 tsp chipotle paste (or chipotles en adobo)
1 tbsp ancho chilli paste
1 tsp cocoa powder
1 tsp light brown soft sugar
500g peeled prawns
butter or ghee, for frying
salt and black pepper

Coleslaw
½ pointed green cabbage
1 large carrot (about 200g)
1 habanero chilli, very finely chopped, if you want it hot, or jalapeño, if you don't
150ml soured cream
1 tsp onion powder
1 tsp garlic powder
1 tsp dried oregano (Mexican oregano if you can get it, otherwise European)
1 tbsp cider vinegar

Mango salsa
1 large mango, peeled and finely diced
1 red onion, finely diced
zest and juice of 1 lime
a few coriander sprigs, finely chopped

To serve
16 tacos
lime wedges

We warn you – these tacos are so good that you'll find it hard to stop eating them. Quite a bit to do here but we've suggested the best order for the prep and none of it is difficult. There should be enough filling for about sixteen small tacos – don't load them up too much or they'll be hard to eat – and that would be a shame.

First start the coleslaw. Put the cabbage and carrot in a colander and set it over a bowl. Sprinkle in half a teaspoon of salt and mix thoroughly. Leave to stand for at least half an hour until the vegetables have released some liquid and have reduced in volume slightly.

Next, marinate the prawns. Put the lime juice and zest, olive oil and chipotle and chilli pastes in a bowl and sprinkle in the cocoa powder and sugar. Season with salt and pepper, then mix thoroughly and add the prawns. Stir to coat them in the mixture, then leave for at least half an hour.

Make the salsa. Mix everything together and season with salt and pepper.

Finish the coleslaw. Transfer the cabbage and carrot to a bowl and add all the remaining ingredients. Mix thoroughly, then taste for seasoning and add more salt and some black pepper if necessary.

Heat the tacos. Line a basket or serving bowl with a tea towel. Heat a dry pan (preferably not non-stick) and heat each taco for a few moments on each side. Place in the lined basket or bowl and cover with the tea towel. Continue until you have heated them all.

Cook the prawns. Drain them as thoroughly as you can, reserving the marinade, and pat them dry. Melt the butter or ghee in a large frying pan over a high heat, then add the prawns. Cook until pink on each side, then remove and keep warm. Add the marinade to the pan and simmer until piping hot. Put the prawns back in the pan and heat them through just before serving.

Fill the tacos. Add some coleslaw to each one, followed by prawns, then the mango salsa and serve with lime wedges.

Our new chicken korma

Serves 4

6 chicken thigh fillets, skinned
    and cut into chunks
1 tsp salt
4 garlic cloves, roughly chopped
20g root ginger, roughly chopped
zest and juice of ½ lime
1 hot green chilli, roughly
    chopped

Sauce
1 tbsp coconut oil or ghee
1 tsp mustard seeds
1 large onion, finely sliced
5 tsp korma spice mix (see p.257)
1 medium tomato (about 100g),
    finely chopped or puréed
2 bay leaves
100g ground almonds or cashews
1 tsp light brown soft sugar
500ml chicken stock
50ml yoghurt or double cream
    (optional)
squeeze of lime
salt and black pepper

To garnish
sliced green chillies, to garnish
handful of coriander, chopped
basmati rice

A good chicken korma is a great favourite of ours. There are many layers of flavour here and we've added a bit of lime zest and juice, which is unusual, but we think it gives a fab twist to the curry. See what you think.

Put the chicken in a bowl and sprinkle over the salt. Put the garlic, ginger, lime zest and chilli into a small food processor with a splash of water and blitz until smooth. Mix the purée with the lime juice and 100ml of water and pour over the chicken, then stir to make sure the chicken is well coated in the mixture. Cover and leave to marinate in the fridge for at least an hour.

Heat the oil or ghee in a large flameproof casserole dish or a lidded sauté pan. Add the mustard seeds and leave them until they start popping, then add the onion slices and cook until they are a light golden brown. Stir in 4 teaspoons of the spice mix, followed by the chicken and any remaining marinade. Cook until the chicken is very lightly coloured on all sides.

Stir in the tomato and add the bay leaves. Cook for 5 minutes, then add the ground almonds or cashews and the sugar. Stir to create a paste, then pour in the stock. Season with salt and pepper.

Bring to the boil, then cover the pan with a lid and turn the heat down to a simmer. Cook for about 25 minutes, stirring regularly and checking that the sauce isn't catching on the bottom of the pan. You should have a thick sauce coating the chicken. Stir in the yoghurt or cream, if using, and check the seasoning. Sprinkle over the remaining spice mix and add a squeeze of lime.

Garnish with the green chillies and coriander, then serve with rice.

Chicken yassa

Serves 4

8 chicken thighs, skin on
    and bone in
2 tbsp groundnut or sunflower oil
4 onions, sliced
3 bay leaves
250ml chicken stock
100g green pitted olives
salt and black pepper

Marinade
1 onion, grated
4 garlic cloves, crushed
15g root ginger, grated
1 scotch bonnet, very finely
    chopped
juice of 1 lemon
2 tbsp red wine vinegar
2 tbsp Dijon mustard

To finish
lemon juice
hot sauce

We're always on the look-out for new curries and this one is simple and really hits the spot. It's our version of chicken yassa, a traditional West African curry that's a fiery mix of mustard, scotch bonnet and ginger. This will warm you up a treat. Nice with some rice.

Mix all the marinade ingredients together in a bowl and season with plenty of salt and pepper. Pour the marinade over the chicken thighs and turn them to coat thoroughly. Cover the bowl, then leave the chicken to marinate in the fridge for several hours, preferably overnight.

Take the chicken out of the fridge an hour before you want to start cooking to allow it to come up to room temperature. Remove the chicken from the marinade and pat it dry. Reserve the marinade for later.

Heat the oil in a wide, flameproof casserole dish or a lidded sauté pan. When the oil is hot, add the chicken, skin-side down, and cook until well browned. Do not rush this stage. Turn the chicken and cook the underside for a few more minutes.

Remove the chicken from the pan and set it aside. Add the onions and bay leaves and cook over a low-medium heat until they are a rich golden brown – it is important to get the onions quite caramelised.

Add the reserved marinade to the pan and cook, stirring regularly for a few minutes until the base of the pan is completely deglazed. Add the stock, then put the chicken back in the pan, skin-side up. Bring to the boil, then turn the heat down and simmer, partially covered, until the chicken is completely cooked through and the sauce has reduced.

Add the olives to the pan and heat through. Check the seasoning and add more salt, pepper, lemon juice or a touch of hot sauce to taste.

Curried beef pasties

Makes 6

500g block of puff pastry
6 dessertspoons of mango
    chutney
1 egg, beaten

Filling
1 tbsp coconut oil
1 large onion, finely chopped
1 small green or red pepper,
    finely diced
1 medium potato (about 150g),
    finely diced
200g beef mince or 200g braising
    steak, very finely diced
2 garlic cloves, finely chopped
1 tbsp medium or hot curry
    powder
1 tbsp tomato purée
1 tsp Worcestershire sauce
2 tbsp coriander stems, finely
    chopped
150ml beef stock
125g frozen peas, defrosted
salt and black pepper

We love a curry and we're big fans of a pasty, so we're really pleased with these spicy little beauties. They're a cross between a Jamaican patty and a Cornish pasty – Kingston meets Kernow! They're made with bought puff pastry, so all you have to do is make the filling and put everything together.

First make the filling. Heat the coconut oil in a large, lidded sauté pan. Add the onion, pepper and potato and cook them over a medium heat until the onion is translucent and starting to take on some colour. Turn up the heat, add the beef and fry until it's well browned. Turn the heat down to medium, then stir in the garlic and cook for another couple of minutes. Stir in the curry powder and the tomato purée and continue to cook, stirring constantly for another 3–4 minutes.

Add the Worcestershire sauce, coriander stems and stock, then season with salt and pepper. Bring to the boil, then cover the pan and leave to simmer until the potatoes are tender. Remove the lid and simmer until the sauce is reduced and thick. Stir in the peas.

Remove the pan from the heat and leave the filling to cool, then transfer it to the fridge to chill. This is important, as you don't want to pile lukewarm filling on to chilled pastry.

When you are ready to assemble the pasties, roll out the pastry as thinly as you can and cut it into 6 rounds measuring about 15cm in diameter. Spread some mango chutney on each round, making sure you leave a good 2cm border around it. Divide the filling between the rounds, placing it in a line down the centre of each. To make sure you do this evenly it's best to weigh the filling and divide it by 6. There will be roughly 100g of filling per pasty.

Brush the exposed pastry border with beaten egg and bring the sides up around the filling so the join is at the top. Crimp the edges together, making sure they are completely sealed, then brush with beaten egg. Place the pasties on a baking tray and chill them for half an hour.

Preheat the oven to 200°C/Fan 180°C/Gas 6. Bake the chilled pasties for 25–30 minutes until crisp and golden brown with a piping hot filling.

Smoky chilli beef & corn crumble

Serves 4

3 tbsp olive oil or lard
700g stewing beef or braising
    steak, diced
150g smoked bacon lardons
2 onions, finely chopped
1 green pepper, diced
2 bay leaves
2 tsp dried oregano
2 tbsp tomato purée
2 tsp chilli powder
1 tsp garlic powder
½ tsp ground allspice
1 tbsp cocoa powder
2 tsp light brown soft sugar
200ml stout (a chocolate
    one is good for this)
200ml beef stock
2 x 400g cans of red kidney
    or pinto beans
salt and black pepper

Crust
175g plain flour
175g medium/coarse cornmeal
1 tsp baking powder
175g butter
75g buttermilk
100g sweetcorn
100g Cheddar cheese, grated

There's nothing as comforting as a crumble, but they don't always have to be for pudding – we both like savoury crumbles as much as sweet ones. This one has a nice Tex-Mex vibe to it with the corn topping and we've included a little cocoa powder in the filling which adds a touch of richness and bitterness that sets the crust off nicely.

Heat half the oil or lard in a large flameproof casserole dish. Season the beef with salt and pepper and sear it until well browned – you will probably have to do this in at least 2 batches. Transfer each batch to a plate and set aside.

Add the remaining oil or lard to the casserole dish, then add the bacon, onions and green pepper. Sauté for a few minutes over a medium-high heat, so the bacon crisps up and the onion takes on some colour, then add the herbs, tomato purée, spices, cocoa and sugar. Stir for a few minutes until a grainy paste forms around the vegetables and the mixture smells rich, slightly caramelised, and spicy.

Add the stout and stock to the casserole dish and deglaze the base thoroughly, scraping up any sticky bits. Put the beef back in the dish and add the beans, then season with plenty of salt and pepper. Bring to the boil, then reduce the heat and partially cover the dish with a lid. Leave to simmer for 1–1½ hours until the beef is tender and the sauce has reduced to a well-flavoured gravy.

Transfer the filling to an ovenproof dish, removing the bay leaves when you find them. Reserve some of the cooking liquid to add at the table if there seems to be too much of it. Preheat the oven to 200°C/Fan 180°C/Gas 6.

To make the crust, put the flour, cornmeal and baking powder into a bowl with a generous pinch of salt. Rub in the butter, then stir in the buttermilk and the mixture should clump together a bit. Stir in the sweetcorn and half the cheese. Sprinkle the mixture over the filling and top with the rest of the grated cheese.

Bake in the oven for 30–35 minutes until the topping is lightly browned and crisp, and the filling is bubbling up underneath.

Caribbean-style pot-roast brisket

Serves 6

1.2–1.5kg rolled brisket
2 tbsp coconut or olive oil
2 onions, roughly chopped
1 carrot, roughly chopped
1 celery stick, roughly chopped
6 garlic cloves, sliced
2 tsp light brown soft sugar
3 tbsp tomato purée
2 large thyme sprigs
2 bay leaves
1–2 scotch bonnets, left whole,
    but pierced with a knife point
1 tsp allspice berries, lightly
    crushed
1 tsp black peppercorns, lightly
    crushed
piece of pared lime zest
500ml beef stock
salt and black pepper

To finish
up to 1 tbsp brandy
squeeze of lime juice
2–3 spring onions, finely sliced
    (include the greens)

Brisket does need long slow cooking but the result is more than worth it – delicious, meltingly soft meat that's packed with flavour. Stick with the Caribbean theme and serve this with rice and peas (see page 253) or fried plantain if you like, or just with some simple mash and veg. Lip-smackingly good.

Season the brisket with salt and pepper. Heat the oil in a flameproof casserole dish just large enough to hold the brisket. Sear the brisket thoroughly on all sides until it has developed a rich brown crust, then remove it and set it aside.

Add the onions, carrot and celery to the dish. Fry over a medium-high heat until they start to take on some colour, then add the garlic. Cook for another couple of minutes, then stir in the sugar and tomato purée. Continue to stir until the sugar has melted and the mixture has a caramelly aroma.

Add the herbs, scotch bonnet(s), spices and lime zest to the pan. Pour over the beef stock and stir to make sure the base of the pan is thoroughly deglazed. Put the brisket back in the pan – the liquid should come about two-thirds of the way up the sides of the meat.

Bring to the boil, then turn the heat down to a simmer. Cover the casserole dish with a lid and cook the beef for at least 3 hours, until it's knife tender but still sliceable – the meat shouldn't be falling apart.

Remove the brisket from the pan and set it aside to keep warm. Strain the liquid into a sieve, pushing through the vegetables to help thicken the gravy. It's up to you whether you include the scotch bonnet as you do so – it will vastly increase the heat of the dish if you do.

Return the strained liquid to the casserole dish and bring it back to the boil. Add a little brandy, a teaspoon at a time, just for flavour, then add the lime juice. Taste for seasoning and add salt, pepper and a little more brandy and lime as necessary.

Slice the brisket, discarding the string as you do so, and arrange the slices on a serving dish or individual plates. Ladle over some of the gravy and garnish with spring onions. Pour any remaining gravy into a jug and serve at the table.

weekend comforts

Breakfast poutine

Serves 4

1.2kg potatoes, cut into wedges
3 tbsp sunflower oil
2 tbsp olive oil
1 large block of halloumi cheese,
    cut into slices
4 eggs
salt and black pepper

Gravy
1 tbsp olive oil
150g smoked bacon, finely diced
1 onion, very finely chopped
1 tsp mustard powder
1 tsp garlic powder
a few small rosemary sprigs, very
    finely chopped
250ml passata
400ml chicken stock
dash of Worcestershire sauce
up to 2 tsp maple syrup (optional)
dash of liquid smoke (optional)

There are all sorts of stories about this dish, but it seems that it originated in Quebec in the 1950s and different versions are now popular throughout Canada. Basically it consists of potatoes and cheese curds topped with rich gravy, so it definitely ticks the comfort food box for us. We've used halloumi cheese, which is easier to get than curds, and we like to top the whole thing with a fried egg. A perfect weekend brunch, lunch or even midnight feast.

First, start the potatoes. Preheat the oven to 200°C/Fan 180°C/Gas 6. Put the potatoes in a pan and cover them with cold water. Bring the water to the boil and simmer for 2 minutes, then drain. Pour the sunflower oil into a large roasting tin and add the potatoes. Toss to coat them in the oil and season with plenty of salt and pepper. Roast them in the oven, shaking the roasting tin every so often, for about 30 minutes.

To make the gravy, heat the olive oil in a sauté pan, add the bacon and fry until crisp. Remove the bacon from the pan, then add the onion and sauté over a medium-high heat until well browned. Put about two-thirds of the bacon back into the pan.

Stir the mustard and garlic powders and the rosemary into the pan, then pour in the passata and chicken stock. Add a dash of Worcestershire sauce and season with salt and pepper, then bring to the boil and simmer for 10 minutes. Taste and add some maple syrup if you think the gravy could do with a touch of sweetness – this will depend on the acidity of the tomatoes. Add a dash of liquid smoke for a smokier flavour, if you like. Continue to simmer the gravy until you are ready to serve.

To fry the halloumi, heat the olive oil in a frying pan and add the halloumi. Fry until it's a rich brown on both sides, then remove, cut into cubes and keep warm. Fry the eggs in the same pan.

To assemble, divide the potatoes between 4 shallow bowls and ladle over some of the gravy. Add some halloumi and a fried egg to each bowl. Warm the reserved bacon in the frying pan, then add it to the bowls. Serve immediately.

Chicory & ham gratin

Serves 4

6–8 heads of chicory, depending
    on size
2 tbsp olive oil
25g butter, plus extra for greasing
50ml white wine or vermouth
leaves from a thyme sprig
6–8 large slices of ham, cut in half
2–3 tbsp Dijon mustard
salt and black pepper

Béchamel sauce
600ml milk
slice of onion
2 bay leaves
4 cloves
1 mace blade
a few peppercorns
40g butter
40g plain flour

Topping
100g hard cheese, such
    as Gruyère, grated

We think this is one of cosiest dishes imaginable – it's so soothing and delicious to eat. We like English or German-style unsmoked ham, not wafer thin but not too thick either or it's hard to wrap around the chicory. You can get this all ready in advance if you like, ready to pop in the oven later and enjoy.

Start by infusing the milk for the béchamel sauce. Pour the milk into a pan and add the onion, bay leaves, cloves, mace blade and peppercorns. Slowly bring the milk almost to the boil, then remove the pan from the heat and leave the milk to infuse for half an hour.

Trim the ends of the heads of chicory, then cut each one in half. Try to make sure the outer leaves are still attached to the core.

Heat half the olive oil in a large sauté pan. When it's hot, add half the chicory pieces, cut-side down, and sear until they are well coloured – aim for a rich, dark-caramel brown. Flip them over, season with salt and pepper, then cook for a few more minutes. Remove the first batch from the pan and repeat with the remaining oil and chicory.

Put the first batch of chicory back in the pan – you should be able to get all the chicory more or less in a single layer now – and add the butter. Pour in the white wine or vermouth and sprinkle over the thyme leaves. Bring to the boil, then lower the heat to medium and cover the pan with a lid. Leave to cook gently for a few minutes until the chicory is tender to the point of a knife. Strain and set the chicory and liquid aside separately.

Take the slices of ham and spread them generously with the mustard. Wrap each piece of chicory in a slice of ham – the chicory doesn't have to be completely encased. Butter an ovenproof dish and arrange the wrapped chicory over the base.

Now finish the sauce. Strain the infused milk into a jug. Heat the butter in a saucepan. Add the flour and stir until the butter and flour are well combined. Continue to cook, stirring constantly, to cook out the raw flavour of the flour, then start adding the milk, a little at a time at first. Make sure the sauce is smooth and lump free after each addition before you add more milk. You should end up with a sauce the consistency of thick pouring cream. Add the leftover juices from cooking the chicory, season the sauce and pour it over the chicory in the dish.

Preheat the oven to 200°C/Fan 180°C/Gas 6. Sprinkle the chicory with cheese, then bake in the oven until the cheese is well browned and the sauce piping hot and bubbling up from underneath.

Spinach & four-cheese lasagne

Serves 4–6

250g cherry tomatoes, quartered
½ tsp dried oregano
12 lasagne sheets
150g Taleggio cheese, roughly torn
100g mozzarella, roughly torn
basil leaves, shredded

Béchamel sauce
800ml milk
1 slice of onion
2 bay leaves
60g butter
60g plain flour

Spinach filling
1 tbsp olive oil
1 onion, finely chopped
1 large courgette, coarsely grated
2 garlic cloves, finely chopped
750g frozen whole leaf spinach, defrosted and drained
50g ricotta
75g Parmesan, finely grated
zest of ½ lemon
a few rasps of nutmeg

Breadcrumb topping
25g fresh breadcrumbs
25g Parmesan, grated
½ tsp oregano
basil leaves, shredded
1 tbsp olive oil

Nothing beats a good lasagne in the comfort stakes and the combination and balance of the cheeses really delivers on flavour. Top tip here is to make sure the vegetables are as dry as possible as you don't want a soggy lasagne. Drain the spinach and tomatoes well and make sure the courgette steams off most of its moisture. A real feast of a dish.

First make the béchamel. Heat the milk with the onion and bay leaves. Bring up to boiling point, then remove the pan from the heat and leave to cool and infuse, then strain. Melt the butter in a saucepan and add the flour. Stir to combine into a roux, then continue to cook and stir for several minutes to cook out the raw flavour of the flour. Add the milk to the roux, a ladleful at a time and stir until the milk is completely combined between each addition and you have a smooth sauce.

Put the cherry tomatoes in a sieve or colander and sprinkle them with salt, then leave them to drain for at least 20 minutes. Sprinkle with the oregano.

To make the spinach filling, heat the olive oil in a sauté pan or frying pan and add the onion. Cook until soft and translucent, then add the courgette and cook until it has reduced down. Stir in the garlic and cook for another minute, then set aside to cool. Roughly chop the spinach and squeeze out as much liquid from it as you can. Add it to the onion and courgette mixture, then add the ricotta, Parmesan, lemon zest and nutmeg. Season with salt and pepper, then stir to combine.

To make the breadcrumb topping, mix the breadcrumbs, Parmesan, oregano and basil together, then drizzle over the olive oil. Toss lightly.

To assemble, spread a small ladleful of the béchamel sauce over the base of a rectangular ovenproof dish. Place 3 lasagne sheets on top, followed by another ladle of the béchamel. Spread a third of the spinach mix over the top and sprinkle over a few of the chopped tomatoes, followed by a quarter of the Taleggio. Top with another layer of lasagne sheets and repeat until you have 3 layers. Add a top layer of lasagne, then pour over the remaining béchamel. Sprinkle over the remaining Taleggio, the mozzarella and a few basil leaves, then top with the breadcrumb mixture.

Preheat the oven to 180°C/Fan 160°C/Gas 4. Bake the lasagne in the oven for 40–45 minutes until the top is brown and bubbling. Remove from the oven and leave to stand and settle for 10–15 minutes before serving.

Aubergine parmigiana

Serves 6

3 large aubergines, thinly sliced
3 large courgettes, cut on the
    diagonal into 5mm slices
50ml olive oil
2 tsp dried oregano
a few rosemary sprigs, finely
    chopped
salt and black pepper

Sauce
2 tbsp olive oil
1 large onion, finely chopped
3 garlic cloves, finely chopped
100ml white wine
1kg ripe fresh tomatoes, peeled
    and roughly chopped or
    2 x 400g cans of chopped
    tomatoes
1 tsp dried oregano
1 large thyme sprig
2 bay leaves

To assemble
2 balls of mozzarella
basil leaves, shredded
50g fine dried breadcrumbs
25g Parmesan, grated

A classic in both our houses, this is our new version of this fabulous dish. Don't be tempted to cut corners here and leave out the salting of the aubergines and courgettes. They will grill or roast much better if the excess water is drained off, trust us. Fresh tomatoes make a lighter, more summery dish but tinned are fine too, so up to you. This makes a lovely supper dish on its own or it's great with some grilled chicken.

Put the aubergines and courgettes in separate colanders if possible and sprinkle a teaspoon of salt over each. Mix them thoroughly with your hands and place the colanders over bowls to catch any liquid. Leave to drain for at least half an hour. Pat the aubergines and courgettes dry, then drizzle with the olive oil, using two-thirds on the aubergines and the rest on the courgettes. Toss with the oregano and rosemary, then season with black pepper.

Preheat the oven to 200°C/Fan 180°C/Gas 6 or heat a large griddle pan. To oven cook, arrange the slices of aubergine and courgette over several baking trays and put them in the oven until well browned. The aubergines will take about 30 minutes, the courgettes about 15 minutes. Alternatively, grill them on a griddle until char lines appear and the slices are softened through.

To make the sauce, heat the oil in a large saucepan and add the onion. Cook over a low-medium heat until soft and translucent, then add the garlic and cook for another couple of minutes.

Turn up the heat and pour in the white wine. Allow it to bubble up until most of it has evaporated, then add the tomatoes and herbs. Season with salt and pepper, then bring to the boil. Turn the heat down to a simmer and cover the pan, then cook for 20 minutes. Remove the lid and leave to simmer and reduce for up to another 30 minutes.

To assemble, pour a little of the sauce into the base of a large ovenproof dish. Add half the aubergines in 1 or 2 layers, a third of the mozzarella and some torn basil. Follow with more sauce, the courgettes, another third of the mozzarella and more basil. Spoon over more sauce, the remaining aubergines and the last of the mozzarella. Pour any remaining sauce on top.

Mix the breadcrumbs and Parmesan together with a few shredded basil leaves. Season with salt and pepper and sprinkle over the top of the dish.

Preheat the oven to 200°C/Fan 180°C/Gas 6. Bake for 30–40 minutes until the top is golden brown and sauce is bubbling up from under the crust. Leave to stand for at least 15 minutes before serving.

Salmon en croûte

Serves 4–6

320g pack of ready-rolled puff
    pastry
2 x 300–350g pieces of salmon
    fillet, skinned
1 egg, beaten
salt and black pepper

Filling
1 tbsp olive oil
15g butter
½ fennel bulb, very finely
    chopped
2 garlic cloves, finely chopped
zest of 1 lemon
100ml white wine
80–100g watercress, very finely
    chopped
2 tsp ouzo or pastis (optional)
100g cream cheese
squeeze of lemon juice

Dill and caper sauce
1 tbsp butter
1 shallot, finely chopped
zest of ½ lemon
1 tsp mustard powder
100ml chicken or fish stock
250ml crème fraiche
small bunch of dill, finely chopped
2 tbsp capers
squeeze of lemon juice

The idea for this came from one of our fishing expeditions when we wanted to do something wonderful with our catch. Whether you call this salmon en croûte or salmon Wellington, it makes a proper fancy dish for a special meal. Salmon, flaky puff pastry and a rich creamy sauce – what more could you want? It's not difficult to make and can all be prepared in advance, so it's the ideal dish for entertaining favourite guests.

First make the filling. Heat the oil and butter in a small frying pan and add the fennel. Sauté over a gentle heat until translucent, then add the garlic and lemon zest. Stir for another minute, then pour in the white wine and season with salt and pepper. Bring to the boil and let the white wine reduce by half, then add the watercress and remove the pan from the heat. Stir until the watercress has wilted, then set aside to cool. Add the ouzo or pastis, if using.

Put the cream cheese in a bowl and season with salt and pepper, then stir in the fennel and watercress mixture. Taste and adjust the seasoning and add a squeeze of lemon juice.

Unroll the pastry and lightly run a rolling pin over it to increase its size by 2–3cm on each side. Place one of the pieces of salmon in the centre of the pastry and season. Spread the filling over the salmon, then season the remaining piece of salmon and place it on top of the filling.

Fold the pastry over the salmon and seal the edges together. Turn the pastry parcel over so the join is underneath and place it on a baking tray. Use a spoon to make a pattern of scales on top of the pastry if you want, then brush with beaten egg. Chill for at least half an hour in the fridge or for 10 minutes in the freezer. You can prepare the salmon ahead to this point and leave it in the fridge for up to 24 hours.

When you are ready to cook, preheat the oven to 220°C/Fan 200°C/Gas 7. Bake the salmon for 15 minutes, then turn the heat down to 180°C/Gas 160°C/Gas 4 and leave to cook for another 25 minutes. Remove the salmon from the oven, then leave it to stand for a few minutes before serving.

While the salmon is baking, make the sauce. Melt the butter in a small saucepan and add the shallot. Sauté until soft and translucent, then stir in the lemon zest and mustard powder. Whisk in the stock and bring to the boil, then simmer for a couple of minutes. Add the crème fraiche, then turn the heat down and heat it through gently. Stir in the dill and capers and season with salt and pepper. Add a squeeze of lemon to cut through the richness.

Slice the salmon into portions and serve with the sauce.

Braised squid

Serves 4

3 tbsp olive oil
600g squid tubes, sliced into rings
3 small red onions, sliced into
    wedges
4 garlic cloves, finely chopped
2 bay leaves
2 large thyme sprigs
2 strips of pared lemon zest
250ml red wine
150ml chicken or vegetable stock
    or water
1 tbsp sherry or red wine vinegar
large pinch of saffron (optional)
600ml new or salad potatoes,
    sliced
400g can of chopped tomatoes
2 red peppers, cut into strips
50g pitted olives
chopped parsley
salt and black pepper

To serve
crusty bread

There's nothing quite like a nice one-pot supper and this squid dish is hearty, tasty and great at any time of year. You might be surprised to see red wine featured in a seafood dish, but it adds depth and richness to the sauce. Squid is easily available in supermarkets now and you can buy it ready-cleaned, so you don't have to mess about. It needs to be cooked either very quickly or slowly for best results so try this slow-cooked version. We think it's really special.

Heat a tablespoon of the oil in a wide, flameproof casserole dish. When it's hot, add half the squid and fry it over a high heat until golden brown. Remove it from the pan and set aside, then add another tablespoon of the olive oil and repeat with the rest of the squid. Set aside.

Add the remaining tablespoon of the oil to the dish, followed by the red onions. Sauté the onions over a medium-high heat until they start to soften. Stir in the garlic, bay leaves, thyme and lemon zest and then put the squid back into the casserole dish. Season with salt and pepper and stir.

Pour over the red wine and bring to the boil. Add the stock or water and the vinegar, bring back to the boil, then cover and simmer for 45 minutes. If including saffron, grind it with a pinch of sea salt using a pestle and mortar, then sprinkle this into the casserole dish.

Add the potatoes and tomatoes and season again, then cover the dish with a lid and continue to cook for another 25 minutes. Arrange the red pepper slices on top, cover again and cook until the red peppers and squid are tender and the potatoes are completely cooked through – this should take about another 20 minutes. Stir in the olives to heat through, then sprinkle with parsley before serving with crusty bread.

Seafood pasta bake

Serves 4

400g short pasta
1 tbsp olive oil
15g butter
2 leeks, finely sliced
2 medium courgettes, diced
3 garlic cloves, finely chopped
leaves from 1 tarragon sprig
zest and juice of 1 lime
100ml white wine
300ml chicken or vegetable stock
200g mascarpone
1 tbsp pastis or ouzo (optional)
200g cooked mixed seafood
200g cooked shelled prawns
50g breadcrumbs
50g Parmesan cheese, grated
a few basil leaves, shredded
salt and black pepper

This tastes really delicious and special, but you can make it with one of those packs of cooked mixed seafood you see in supermarket chiller cabinets, plus some cooked prawns. Put these together with some pasta, veg and an easy mascarpone sauce and you have a supper to be proud of.

Cook the pasta in plenty of well-salted, boiling water until just al dente. Reserve a couple of ladlefuls of the cooking water, drain the pasta and then set it aside.

Heat the olive oil and butter in a flameproof casserole dish. Add the leeks and courgettes and fry them over a medium heat for about 5 minutes until they are starting to soften. Add the garlic, tarragon and lime zest. Season with salt and pepper, then pour in the white wine and stock. Bring to the boil, then turn the heat down to a simmer and leave the vegetables to braise for a few minutes until tender.

Add the mascarpone and stir until it has formed a smooth, creamy sauce around the vegetables. Stir in the pastis or ouzo, if using, followed by the mixed seafood, prawns and pasta. Stir to combine and add a little of the pasta water if you think you need a little more sauce – it will thicken as it bakes. Taste and add lime juice and more seasoning if necessary.

Preheat the oven to 200°C/Fan 180°C/Gas 6. Mix the breadcrumbs, Parmesan and basil leaves together and sprinkle over the pasta. Bake in the preheated oven for 20–25 minutes until the top is crisp and brown and the pasta is bubbling up underneath. Sprinkle with basil leaves and serve.

Chicken potstickers

Makes about 25

packet of gyoza wrappers or make
    your own (see p.264)
vegetable oil

Filling
2 tsp vegetable or olive oil
50g Chinese lettuce, very finely
    shredded and chopped
50g carrot, grated or cut into
    matchsticks and chopped
10g root ginger, finely chopped
2 garlic cloves, finely chopped
pinch of Chinese 5-spice powder
200g minced chicken
3 spring onions, finely chopped
1 tsp sesame oil
salt and black pepper

Dipping sauce
2 tbsp dark soy sauce
1 tbsp rice wine vinegar
1 tbsp chilli oil (or to taste)
1 tsp sesame oil
½ tsp caster sugar

To serve
soy sauce
chilli sauce

Potstickers – part-fried, part-steamed Chinese dumplings – are a comfort classic for us. We've done a vegetarian recipe in the past and loved that so much we thought we'd go for a chicken version. If you buy wrappers, make sure you get the ones for gyozas, not dumplings, as the gyoza ones are thinner. The ultimate TV dinner, this goes down a treat with a cold beer.

To make the filling, heat the oil in a frying pan and sauté the lettuce and carrot until they have wilted down. Stir in the ginger and garlic and cook for another couple of minutes, then sprinkle with Chinese 5-spice powder. Remove the pan from the heat and leave to cool.

Put the chicken into a bowl and season with salt and black pepper. Stir in the cooled lettuce and carrot mixture, spring onions and sesame oil, then mix together thoroughly.

To assemble the dumplings, put a heaped teaspoon of filling in the centre of a gyoza wrapper. Wet around the sides – be thorough, as the wrappers can sometimes crack – then pinch the edges together, pleating from the middle down each side to seal. Repeat to use up all the filling.

Mix the dipping sauce ingredients together until the sugar has dissolved. Taste for seasoning and add salt if necessary.

To cook, heat some vegetable oil in a non-stick, lidded frying pan – you need just enough to thinly cover the base. Add some of the dumplings, making sure they are well spread out. Fry over a medium heat until they are crisp and brown underneath, then add water – again, just enough to thinly cover the base of the pan. Cover and steam the dumplings for 5 minutes until they are starting to look translucent and the water has evaporated. Cook for another minute, uncovered, to make sure the underside is still crisp.

Serve hot with the dipping sauce and some extra soy sauce and chilli sauce to add at the table.

Skirlie-stuffed chicken

Serves 6

1 x 1.5–1.8kg oven-ready chicken
1 large onion, sliced into thick
    rounds
1 thyme sprig
25g butter
squeeze of lemon juice
salt and black pepper

Skirlie stuffing
50g butter or dripping
1 large onion, finely chopped
a few sage leaves, finely chopped
a few parsley sprigs, finely
    chopped
125g oatmeal (medium or coarse)
    or pinhead oats
100ml chicken stock
1 egg, beaten

Gravy
1 tbsp flour
100ml white wine
300ml chicken stock

When asked for their favourite comfort meals, many people will include roast chicken on the list. It's one of those dishes that means home and family and warmth. We've given this classic roast a Scottish slant with an oatmeal stuffing known as skirlie, which soaks up juices and flavour from the chicken and adds another level of deliciousness to a Sunday roast. Do try this it's excellent and a bit different.

If possible, the day before you want to roast your chicken, remove it from any packaging and put it on a plate. Sprinkle with salt, then place it in the fridge, uncovered or loosely wrapped in kitchen paper. This helps to make the skin really crispy. Remove the chicken from the fridge at least an hour before you want to start roasting it.

To make the stuffing, melt the butter in a frying pan and add the onion. Fry it over a medium-high heat until softened and starting to brown, then stir in the herbs and oatmeal or oats. Season with salt and plenty of black pepper – add more than you think you need! Pour over the chicken stock, then cook gently for 15–20 minutes, stirring regularly, until the oatmeal has cooked to an al dente texture. It will be quite crumbly and dry looking. Remove from the heat and leave to cool, then stir in the egg.

Preheat the oven to 220°C/Fan 200°C/Gas 7.

Stuff the skirlie into the main cavity of the chicken, then weigh the stuffed chicken so you can work out how long to cook it for. Arrange the onion slices in the centre of a roasting tin and add the thyme., then place the chicken on top. Spread the butter over the chicken and sprinkle over the lemon juice.

Roast the chicken for 15 minutes, then reduce the oven temperature to 180°C/Fan 160°C/Gas 4. Cook the chicken for 20 minutes per 500g. When the cooking time is up, check for doneness. A temperature probe should read 72°C in the centre of the stuffing and in the thickest part of the leg and any juices should run clear. The legs will also feel loose.

Remove the chicken from the roasting tin along with the onions and cover loosely with foil. Pour the pan juices into a jug, then sprinkle the flour over the roasting tin. Place over a low heat and stir to scrape up any brown bits on the base of the tin – the flour will form a roux with any fat. Add the white wine and bring it to the boil, stirring to make sure the roasting tin base is completely clean. Transfer to a saucepan, add the stock and any juices from the resting chicken and simmer until you have a reduced gravy. Serve with the chicken and stuffing.

Fried chicken

Serves 4

8 chicken pieces (thighs and
     drumsticks), bone in and
     skin on
juice of 1 lemon
300ml buttermilk
2 large thyme sprigs, lightly
     bruised
100g plain flour
50g cornflour
1 tsp baking powder
vegetable oil or beef dripping
salt and black pepper

Spice mix
1 tbsp garlic powder
2 tsp smoked paprika
2 tsp mustard powder
1 tsp oregano
1 tsp cayenne

*Tender and juicy, our fried chicken really is finger-licking good.
It's easy too – no deep-frying, no faffing about transferring
partially cooked chicken to the oven, just simply frying in two
steps which works brilliantly. This is a cracking recipe.*

First make the spice mix. Mix all the spices together and add plenty of black
pepper and a teaspoon of salt.

Put the chicken in a bowl, add the lemon juice and toss the chicken in it. Whisk
half of the spice mix into the buttermilk and add the thyme. Pour this mixture
over the chicken and stir to make sure the chicken is completely coated.
Cover the bowl and leave the chicken to marinate for at least 4 hours in the
fridge or overnight.

Whisk the remaining spice mix with the plain flour, cornflour and baking
powder, then add a teaspoon of salt.

Remove the chicken from the marinade and place it on a rack to dry slightly
and come up to room temperature. Dip the chicken pieces in the flour
mixture, making sure they are thoroughly coated.

Heat some oil or dripping in a large, lidded frying pan – the oil or fat should be
at least 1cm deep. Keep the heat to medium-high – if it's too hot, the coating
will burn before the chicken is cooked through. Place the chicken in the frying
pan, skin-side down for thighs, and cover with a lid. Cook for 5–6 minutes on
each side until the chicken is lightly golden and just cooked through. Turn up
the heat and fry for 2–3 minutes more on each side until the chicken is darker
brown in colour and crisp.

Drain on kitchen paper, blotting both sides of the chicken pieces. Set them
aside for 5 minutes before serving with salad and perhaps a dip.

Duck confit shepherd's pie

Serves 4

2 confit duck legs (shop-bought
   or see p.256)
1 large onion, finely chopped
1 large carrot, finely diced
150g celeriac, finely diced
250g mushrooms, such as
   portobellini, diced
4 garlic cloves, finely chopped
1 large thyme sprig
2 bay leaves
250ml red wine
200ml chicken stock
800g floury potatoes, sliced
100g Comté or Gruyère cheese,
   grated
salt and black pepper

Duck confit is simply duck legs cooked slowly in duck fat until the meat is meltingly soft and tender, and we've used it in this recipe to make one of the tastiest and most luxurious shepherd's pies you've ever eaten. Duck confit is very popular in France but even there, lots of people tend to buy it ready-made rather than make their own. We've added a recipe in case you do want to start from scratch, but otherwise this pie will be great with shop-bought confit. We've suggested a sliced potato topping, but it's fine to use regular mash if you prefer.

Scrape the fat off the duck legs. Put the duck legs in a frying pan and fry them gently on both sides, just long enough to melt off the fat and crisp up the skin. Remove them from the frying pan and pull the meat into chunks, discarding any bone and cartilage. Set the fat aside.

Take a tablespoon of the duck fat and heat it in a flameproof casserole dish. Add the onion, carrot and celeriac and fry them for a few minutes until they're starting to brown. Add the mushrooms and continue to fry until they are browned and any liquid they release has evaporated off.

Add the duck meat to the casserole dish along with the garlic. Stir for a couple of minutes, then add the herbs. Pour over the wine and bring to the boil. Allow the wine to reduce by half, then add the chicken stock.

Bring the mixture back to the boil, then turn down the heat and leave it to simmer, partially covered, for 20 minutes. Meanwhile, put the potatoes in a steamer basket and season them with salt. Steam for 5 minutes – they should be partially cooked in this time and starting to soften, but not breaking up.

Preheat the oven to 200°C/Fan 180°C/Gas 6. Arrange the potato slices over the duck mixture, then sprinkle with the grated cheese. Bake in the preheated oven for 25–30 minutes until the potatoes are completely tender and the cheese has browned.

Rigatoni pie

Serves 6–8

Meat sauce
2 tbsp olive oil
1 onion, finely chopped
1 small carrot, finely chopped
1 celery stick, finely chopped
3 garlic cloves, finely chopped
400g beef mince
1 tsp dried oregano
leaves from a thyme sprig
½ tsp chilli flakes (optional)
2 bay leaves
150ml red wine
400g can of tomatoes, puréed
salt and black pepper

Pasta
500g rigatoni
1 tbsp olive oil
35g Parmesan cheese,
    very finely grated

To assemble
small bunch of basil leaves
3 x 125g balls of mozzarella
25g Parmesan, grated

We came across a pasta pie like this when filming in Italy one time. It sounds barmy but it's a bit of a show-stopper and a whole different way of serving pasta and meat sauce. Basically, you stand the little tubes of cooked pasta upright in a cake tin, then pour over the sauce to fill the tubes. Top with mozzarella and Parmesan and you have a delicious, very hearty feast.

First make the meat sauce. Heat the oil in a saucepan and add the onion, carrot and celery. Cook the vegetables over a low-medium heat until soft and translucent but don't let them take on any colour. Add the garlic and cook for another couple of minutes.

Turn up the heat and add the beef mince. Fry it briskly until well browned, then season with plenty of salt and pepper. Stir in the oregano, thyme, chilli flakes, if using, and bay leaves, then pour over the red wine. Bring to the boil and leave for a few minutes until most of the wine has evaporated off, then add the tomatoes. Swill the tin out with 200ml of water and add it to the pan.

Bring the mixture to the boil, then reduce the heat, cover the pan and leave to simmer for 20 minutes. Remove the lid and continue to simmer, uncovered, for another 10–15 minutes until the sauce has reduced down a little. Remove the bay leaves, then, using a stick blender, purée the sauce very lightly, just enough to break up any clumps of meat.

Cook the rigatoni in plenty of salted water until it is al dente – be sure not to overcook it or it will be harder to arrange in the tin. Drain the pasta and toss it lightly in the olive oil, then in the grated Parmesan, trying to make sure the coating is as even as possible.

Preheat the oven to 200°C/Fan 180°C/Gas 6 and lightly oil a 23cm springform cake tin. Arrange the rigatoni in the tin so each piece of pasta is standing upright. Add basil leaves at intervals – they should stick easily to the rigatoni. Make sure the rigatoni are fitting together snugly, then start pouring over the sauce. Do this very gradually so you can see what you are doing – if you pour the sauce over all at once, you won't find it easy to tell which tubes still need filling. Make sure the sauce fills the tubes to the brim – if necessary, poke the sauce down with the end of a chopstick. There should be enough sauce left to coat the top of the pasta.

Tear the mozzarella into pieces and place it over the pasta and sauce, then sprinkle over the Parmesan. Bake the pie in the oven for about 30 minutes, until piping hot. Leave it to rest at room temperature for about 10–15 minutes to let it set, then place the tin on a large serving plate. Run a palette knife around the edge of the tin, then remove the sides. You should find that the pie keeps its shape. Serve immediately, perhaps with a green salad.

Tartiflette pie

Serves 6

1.5kg Charlotte potatoes
(or waxy potatoes), diced
1 tbsp olive oil
15g butter
1 large onion, finely chopped
200g bacon lardons
3 garlic cloves, finely chopped
leaves from a large thyme sprig
150ml white wine
200ml whipping cream
75g hard cheese, such as Cheddar
or Comté, grated
200g soft, rinded cheese, such as
a Somerset brie, thinly sliced
1 x 320g pack of puff pastry
1 egg, beaten
salt and black pepper

A traditional tartiflette is made of bacon, potatoes, cheese and cream and if that wasn't wonderful enough, we decided to take things a step further and add a lid of puff pastry! This is Alpine comfort food with a double dose of deliciousness.

Bring a large saucepan of water to the boil and add salt. Add the potatoes and boil them for 5 minutes. Drain thoroughly.

Heat the olive oil and butter in a large frying pan. Add the onion and bacon and sauté over a medium heat until the bacon is crisp and brown and the onion has started to caramelise.

Add the potatoes and cook for another few minutes over a high heat until they have taken on plenty of flavour from the onion and bacon. Stir in the garlic and thyme and cook for another couple of minutes. Pour in the wine and bring to the boil, then allow it to bubble until the wine has reduced by half. Remove the pan from the heat, then stir in the cream, followed by the grated hard cheese. Season with plenty of salt and pepper.

Butter a large ovenproof dish and pour in half the potato mixture. Arrange the slices of soft cheese on top, then add the rest of the potato mix, spreading it out evenly. Leave to cool completely.

Preheat the oven to 200°C/Fan 180°C/Gas 6. Roll out the puff pastry to fit the dish. Place it over the potato mixture and brush it with beaten egg. Cut a couple of slits in the top.

Bake the pie in the oven for about 25 minutes until the pastry is puffed up and golden, and the filling is piping hot.

Pork & bean casserole

Serves 4

500g haricot beans, soaked
    overnight in salted water
2 small onions, peeled but left
    whole
6 cloves
1 carrot, thickly sliced
3 bay leaves
1 large thyme sprig
4 garlic cloves, left whole
2 tbsp olive oil
8 large sausages or 12 chipolatas
500g pork belly, diced
150g smoked bacon lardons
150ml red wine
2 tbsp tomato purée
1–2 tbsp Dijon mustard
1–2 tsp light brown soft sugar
1–2 tbsp treacle
up to 1 tbsp cider vinegar
    (optional)
salt and black pepper

You don't have to be a cowboy to enjoy this one. We like to think of it as a sort of cross between a cassoulet and Boston baked beans. It's the ideal big hug of a dish to enjoy on a winter weekend when it's snowing outside and spring seems far away.

Drain the soaked beans, then transfer them to a large saucepan and cover them with water. Add a teaspoon of salt and plenty of pepper. Stud the onions with the cloves and add them to the pan, together with the carrot, bay leaves, thyme and garlic.

Bring to the boil, then cover the pan and leave the beans to simmer for about 45 minutes. At this point, the beans should be well on their way to being tender but still quite firm.

While the beans are cooking, heat a tablespoon of the olive oil in a large frying pan and fry the sausages on all sides. Remove them from the pan and set them aside, then add the remaining olive oil. Add the diced pork belly and sear until well browned, then remove it from the pan and quickly fry the bacon lardons.

Pour the wine into the pan with the bacon and stir to deglaze the base of the frying pan. Stir in the tomato purée and half of the mustard, sugar and treacle.

Pour the bacon and wine mixture into the saucepan of beans, along with the pork. Slice the sausages and add them too. Partially cover the pan and continue to cook for up to another hour and a half, until the pork is completely tender, and the liquid has reduced to a thick sauce.

Taste and adjust the seasoning as you like – you may need more mustard, sugar or treacle. You can also add some cider vinegar, a teaspoon at time, if you want a bit of sharpness to cut through the richness.

Take the onions and garlic out of the pan. Remove the cloves from the onions and pull the onions apart. Squash the flesh out of the garlic cloves and stir it and the onions into the pork and beans. Serve piping hot.

Roast pork belly

Serves 4

1kg piece of pork belly,
off the bone and scored
1 tbsp vegetable oil
16 baby onions, peeled and
blanched for 1 minute
3 garlic cloves, finely chopped
2 red chillies, sliced
4 star anise, broken up
3 tbsp preserved lemon, finely
chopped
1 tbsp light brown soft sugar
250ml just-boiled water
1 tbsp plain flour
100ml white wine
250ml chicken or pork stock
a squeeze of lemon juice
(optional)
salt and black pepper

Meltingly tender meat and crisp, crunchy skin – that's what makes pork belly such a treat. We've added star anise and preserved lemon to this recipe, which brings lovely depth and flavour to the meat – and the gravy. Serve this up for Sunday dinner and the family will be mega happy.

Preheat the oven to 160°C/Fan 140°C/Gas 3. Put the pork in a heatproof dish, then bring a kettle of water to the boil and carefully pour the boiling water over the pork belly. Pat it dry and drizzle with the vegetable oil. Rub the oil evenly on to the pork skin, then sprinkle liberally with salt.

Arrange the onions over the centre of a large roasting tin, then sprinkle over the garlic, chillies, star anise, preserved lemon and sugar. Place the pork on top and add the 250ml of freshly boiled water to the roasting tin.

Put the pork in the oven and roast it for about 2½ hours, checking regularly and adding more water to the tin if it looks as though the base is getting dry – you don't want anything to burn.

After 2½ hours, turn the oven temperature up to 220°C/Fan 200°C/Gas 7 and roast for another 20–30 minutes to crisp up the skin. When the skin looks crisp, dry and slightly blistered, remove the pork from the oven and keep it warm on a platter.

Remove the onions from the roasting tin and add them to the platter with the pork. Strain off the pan juices and set them aside to cool. Stir the flour into the roasting tin to form a thick paste, then add the wine. Set the tin over a high heat and let the wine bubble up, while stirring constantly to deglaze the bottom of the roasting tin.

Add the stock and when the base of the roasting tin is completely clean, pour everything into a small saucepan. Skim the reserved pan juices of any fat – which should have risen to the top and quickly set – and add the juices to the gravy. Simmer the gravy until you are ready to serve, then taste and adjust the seasoning, adding a squeeze of lemon juice if you think the gravy needs it. Strain the gravy into a jug to remove the star anise, then serve it with the pork and onions.

Szechuan lamb bao buns

Serves 4

1kg lamb shoulder, on the bone
15g root ginger, very finely sliced
4 garlic cloves, very finely sliced
1 tbsp vegetable oil
salt and black pepper

Rub
1 tbsp Szechuan peppercorns
1 tbsp cumin powder
1 tbsp Chinese 5-spice powder
1 tsp chilli powder
1 tbsp light brown soft sugar
    or honey
1 tbsp rice vinegar
2 tbsp dark soy sauce
1 tsp salt

Sauce
1 tbsp honey or light brown
    soft sugar
2 tbsp dark soy sauce
2 tbsp mirin/rice wine
1 tbsp rice wine vinegar

To serve
1 tbsp rice wine vinegar
1 tsp caster sugar
1 large carrot, cut into
    matchsticks
12 small or 8 medium bao buns
    (see p.265 or shop-bought)
4 spring onions, halved
    lengthways and finely
    shredded
a small bunch of coriander
leaves from a small bunch of mint

Quite a bit to do here but you'll know it was all worthwhile when you bite into a pillowy bao bun filled with meltingly tender lamb and fragrant sauce. Heaven! You can buy the buns in supermarkets, but you'll find a recipe on page 265 if you want to make your own – they are really easy and well worth doing. A truly fantastic dish.

Preheat the oven to 160°C/Fan 140°C/Gas 3. To make the rub, roughly crush the Szechuan peppercorns using a pestle and mortar, then mix with all the other rub ingredients to make a paste. Cut slits all over the lamb. Push slivers of the ginger and garlic into the slits, then liberally coat all sides of the lamb with the paste, pushing some of it into the slits too. Place the lamb in a roasting tin and pour 500ml of water around it. Cover the tin with foil and place it in the oven.

Roast the lamb for about 4 hours, or until the meat is tender and pulls apart easily. Test by pulling on the bone – if it starts to come away very easily and cleanly, the lamb should be tender. Start checking after 3 hours. Remove the lamb from the oven and shred the meat with a couple of forks, removing any large pieces of fat.

To make the sauce, whisk all the ingredients together and taste for seasoning. Add salt and pepper as necessary.

Heat a frying pan and add the oil. Add the shredded lamb, then drizzle over 3 tablespoons of the sauce. Heat through until the sauce has reduced around the lamb and started to caramelise.

To make a carrot garnish, put the rice wine vinegar and sugar in a bowl with half a teaspoon of salt and mix until the sugar has dissolved. Add the carrots and toss to combine.

For the bao buns, prepare a steamer. When the water is boiling, add the buns, still on their parchment, to the steamer basket – you will probably have to do this in 2 or 3 batches, depending on the size of the steamer. It's fine for the buns to touch, but make sure they aren't squashed together. Steam the buns for 8–10 minutes until cooked through and puffed up.

Serve the lamb in the buns with more of the sauce drizzled over and garnish with the carrot, spring onions, coriander and mint.

Meatballs with braised peas & broad beans

Serves 4

Meatballs
2 tbsp olive oil
1 onion, finely chopped
4 garlic cloves, finely chopped
600g lamb mince
50g breadcrumbs
1 egg
1 tsp dried mint
2 tsp ras-el-hanout
zest of 1 lemon
25g dried apricots, soaked
    in warm water and finely
    chopped
salt and black pepper

Vegetables
2 tbsp olive oil
1 large onion, diced
3 garlic cloves, finely chopped
zest of 1 lemon
100ml white wine
300ml chicken or vegetable stock
1 large tomato, puréed
300g frozen peas, defrosted
300g frozen broad beans,
    defrosted
leaves from a small bunch of mint
a small bunch coriander, finely
    chopped
100g hard cheese such as
    Cheddar, grated

The peas and beans give this dish a lighter more summery feel than usual for a meatball recipe and it's packed with flavour. It's fine to use frozen peas and beans and there's no need to defrost them first. Nice with some buttered new potatoes.

For the meatballs, heat half the oil in a frying pan and add the onion. Sauté until soft and translucent, then add the garlic. Cook for another couple of minutes, then remove the pan from the heat and leave to cool.

Put the lamb into a bowl along with all the remaining ingredients and the cooled onion and garlic. Mix thoroughly, then divide into 12 meatballs. Heat the remaining oil in a large frying pan and fry the meatballs briefly to give them some colour. Remove from the heat.

For the vegetables, heat the olive oil in a shallow flameproof casserole dish and add the onion. Sauté the onion for several minutes until it's starting to turn translucent, then add the garlic and lemon zest. Stir for a couple of minutes to coat them in the oil, then pour over the white wine and stock. Stir in the tomato and season with salt and pepper. Bring to the boil and cover the pan, then turn down the heat and leave to simmer for 5 minutes.

Add the peas and broad beans, then add the meatballs, pushing them into the vegetables. Cover and simmer for 20 minutes – the aim is for soft, sweet peas. Preheat a grill and sprinkle the meatballs with the herbs and cheese. Place the dish under the grill for a few minutes until the cheese has browned and the mixture is bubbling, then serve.

Lamb & caper pie

Serves 6

1kg lamb shoulder, trimmed
    of fat and diced
1 tbsp plain flour
1 tbsp mustard powder
3–4 tbsp olive oil
1 onion, finely chopped
1 large carrot, finely diced
2 celery sticks, finely diced
100ml white wine
1 large thyme sprig
2 bay leaves
2 rosemary sprigs
300ml chicken stock
1 large piece of pared lemon zest
4 tbsp capers, drained
salt and black pepper

Pastry
300g plain flour, plus extra
    for dusting
75g butter, chilled and diced
75g lard, chilled and diced
    (or another 75g butter)
1 egg, beaten

We once won a cooking competition with our lamb and caper pudding, so thought we would take things a step further. There's nothing better than a pie for a special weekend feast and this one is sensational. The filling is rich and flavourful and the capers add a nice touch of sharpness. This is a winner.

Season the lamb with salt and pepper, then toss it in the flour and mustard powder. Heat a tablespoon of the olive oil in a large flameproof casserole dish. When the oil is hot, sear the lamb on all sides until it has a good crust. It's best to do this in batches so you don't overcrowd the pan. Place each batch on a plate and add a little more oil to the casserole dish with each batch.

Add any remaining oil to the casserole dish. Sauté the onion, carrot and celery over a low-medium heat until lightly coloured, stirring frequently. Turn up the heat again and pour in the white wine. Stir vigorously to deglaze the base of the dish, then add the herbs. Put the lamb back in the casserole dish and pour over the chicken stock, then season again and tuck in the piece of lemon zest.

Bring to the boil, then turn down the heat, put a lid on the dish and leave the filling to cook for at least an hour. The meat should be tender but if not, cook it for a little longer – up to another half an hour, if necessary. Using a slotted spoon, remove the lamb from the casserole dish and set it aside. Strain the liquid and vegetables through a sieve into a saucepan, pushing as much of the veg through the sieve as possible – this purée will help to thicken the gravy. Pour the liquid back into the casserole dish, then chop 2 tablespoons of the capers and stir them in. Leave the lamb to cool separately.

To make the pastry for the pie crust, put the flour in a bowl with a pinch of salt and add the butter and lard, if using. Rub the fat in until the mixture resembles fine breadcrumbs, then add all but a tablespoon of the egg. Add just enough cold water to form a dough. You shouldn't need more than a couple of tablespoons, but make sure your pastry isn't crumbly.

Dust a work surface with flour, roll out two-thirds of the pastry and use it to line a large pie dish. Wrap the remaining pastry and put that and the lined pie dish into the fridge to chill for at least half an hour.

Preheat the oven to 200°C/Fan 180°C/Gas 6. Mix the lamb with the remaining capers, left whole, and pile it all into the pie dish. Ladle over some of the gravy, just to moisten. Mix the reserved egg with a tablespoon of water and brush the exposed pastry. Roll out the remaining pastry and lay it over the filling. Trim the edges and crimp them together, then cut a couple of steam holes in the top and brush with the rest of the egg. Bake the pie in the oven for about 40 minutes until the filling is piping hot and the pastry is golden. Reheat the gravy to serve with the pie at the table.

Beef short ribs

Serves 4

4 large or 8 small beef short ribs
1 tbsp olive oil
15g butter
2 onions, thickly sliced
4 garlic cloves, sliced
2 bay leaves
1 large thyme sprig
250ml beer
225ml ginger beer

Rub
1 tbsp garlic powder
1 tbsp mustard powder
1 tbsp ground ginger
1 tbsp cocoa powder
2 tsp smoked paprika
1 tsp cayenne
1 tsp ground cumin
1 tsp dried oregano
1 tsp salt
2 tbsp groundnut or sunflower oil

To finish
100ml ginger beer
25ml bourbon (optional)
1 tbsp light soy sauce
1 tbsp cider vinegar
liquid smoke, to taste (optional)
dash of hot sauce, to taste
    (optional)

Ribs have always been a great favourite of mine and my mam used to make the best flat rib beef broth when I was a kid. I still love to cook ribs in all sorts of ways and the meat eaters in my family are big fans of this recipe. Every morsel vanishes in no time and Hardy, the dog, is quite happy with the bones at the end, so everyone's a winner. (Si)

First make the rub. Put the spices into a bowl with the salt and oil. Mix thoroughly, then coat the short ribs with the rub. Cover and leave them to marinate in the fridge for a few hours or preferably overnight.

Heat the olive oil in a large flameproof casserole dish and sear the ribs until well browned. Remove the ribs and add the butter. As soon as it has foamed, add the onions and sauté them over a medium heat until golden brown, stirring regularly. Add the garlic and stir for another couple of minutes.

Add the bay leaves, thyme, beer and ginger beer. Stir to make sure the base of the dish is deglazed and bring to the boil. Turn down the heat and put the ribs back in the casserole dish. Cover and simmer the ribs over the lowest of heats for 2 hours. By this time, the meat should be quite tender and will have shrunk a little around the ribs.

Remove the ribs from the dish and strain the remaining liquid into a jug or gravy separator. Put the ribs back in the dish and cover with a lid – the residual heat should keep them warm while you make the sauce. Skim the fat off the cooking liquid and discard it.

Put 250ml of the cooking liquid in a saucepan and cook until reduced by half. Add the 100ml of ginger beer and simmer again until the liquid has reduced by half. Add the bourbon, if using, the soy sauce and the cider vinegar. If using the liquid smoke, add a few drops at a time until you get a nice smokiness. Taste for seasoning and add a dash of hot sauce if you would like the sauce to have more heat. Continue to simmer until syrupy and taste for seasoning.

Preheat a grill to medium-high, heat a griddle pan on your hob or prepare a barbecue. Brush the ribs liberally with the sauce and grill for a few minutes on both sides until lightly charred and heated through. Serve the ribs with more of the sauce.

teatime

Glamorgan sausage rolls

Makes 24

Filling
15g butter
2 leeks, finely chopped
leaves from a thyme sprig
leaves from a tarragon sprig
100g breadcrumbs
150g hard cheese, such as
    Caerphilly, Cheddar
    or Gruyère, grated
3 egg yolks
1 tsp English mustard
3 tbsp milk
1 tsp Worcestershire sauce

To assemble
1 x 320g pack of ready-rolled
    puff pastry
1 egg, beaten

To serve
chilli relish (see p.260)

Don't ignore the old favourites – these are the original veggie sausages and they're really tasty. Vegetarians will love them – and so will everyone else. The filling is easy to make, but you do need a good strong cheese to get the flavour. Serve as they are or with our delicious chilli relish. Great for a picnic too.

First make the filling. Melt the butter in a frying pan and add the leeks. Stir in the thyme and tarragon, then sauté the leeks over a gentle heat until soft and translucent. Transfer them to a bowl and leave to cool.

Add all the remaining ingredients to the bowl and mix thoroughly. You should end up with a slightly sticky mixture – if it's at all crumbly, add a little more milk. Chill for half an hour. Preheat the oven to 200°C/Fan 180°C/Gas 6.

To assemble, unroll the puff pastry and cut it in half, lengthways.

Divide the filling in half and roll each piece into a sausage the same length as the pastry. Place each sausage down the middle of a piece of pastry.

Brush the exposed edge of the pastry with the beaten egg, then fold the pastry over the filling and seal the edges. Cut each roll into 12 pieces.

Arrange the rolls on 2 baking sheets and brush them with beaten egg. Bake in the preheated oven for 25–30 minutes until the pastry is crisp and golden brown and the filling is piping hot. Good hot or cold.

Mushroom & bacon toast topper

Serves 4

1 tbsp olive oil

4 rashers of streaky bacon,
    finely chopped

25g butter

1 shallot or small onion, very
    finely chopped

500g mushrooms, sliced

3 garlic cloves, grated or crushed

leaves from a large tarragon sprig,
    finely chopped

leaves from a thyme sprig

1 tsp Dijon mustard

200ml chicken stock

100ml cream cheese

squeeze of lemon juice (optional)

a few chives, finely chopped,
    to garnish

salt and black pepper

To serve

4 large slices of sourdough bread,
    toasted and buttered

There's nothing so comforting as something tasty on toast and we both used to love toast toppers from a tin as kids. The idea was great but our recipe for a home-made version is a cracker. You could also serve the topping mix with pasta or spoon it over baked potatoes.

Heat the olive oil in a large frying pan. Add the bacon and fry it until crisp and well browned. Remove the bacon from the pan and place it on some kitchen paper to drain.

Heat the butter in the same pan. When it has completely melted and started to foam, add the shallot or onion and sauté until soft and translucent. Turn up the heat and add the mushrooms. Season them with salt and pepper, then cook, stirring regularly, until they are browned and quite dry.

Add the garlic and herbs to the pan and cook for another couple of minutes, then stir in the mustard and chicken stock. Simmer for 3–4 minutes to reduce the liquid, then stir in the cream cheese. You should end up with a creamy sauce around the mushrooms.

Put most of the bacon back in the pan and stir to warm it through. Taste for seasoning and adjust as necessary. Add a little lemon juice if you want the sauce slightly sharper.

Pile the mixture on to slices of toast and garnish with the rest of the bacon and the chives.

White beans on toast

Serves 4

1 tbsp olive oil

3 garlic cloves, finely chopped

2 x 250g cans of cannellini beans,
    drained (or 500g cooked white
    beans)

salt and black pepper

Sauce

40g basil leaves

zest and juice of 1 lemon

2 tbsp olive oil

25g Parmesan cheese, grated

To serve

4 large slices of sourdough bread,
    toasted

1 garlic clove, halved

butter, for spreading

4 medium tomatoes, thinly sliced

1 red onion, finely sliced and
    sprinkled with salt

basil leaves

*Unbelievably simple and beautifully rich and creamy, this is a
perfect teatime treat or a nourishing snack at any time of day.
The tomato and onion help to cut through the richness and add
a nice pop of colour.*

First make the sauce. Put the basil, zest and juice in a small food processor or
blender and blitz until smooth. Add the olive oil and cheese and continue to
process to make a creamy green sauce. Add salt and black pepper to taste.

Heat the olive oil in a pan and add the garlic. Cook for a minute or so, then stir
in the beans and add just a splash of water. Heat the beans through and season
them with salt and pepper. Add the sauce to the pan and allow it to warm
through briefly, then remove the pan from the heat.

While the beans are heating, toast the bread. Rub the halves of garlic over the
slices of toast, then spread with butter. Arrange the sliced tomatoes over the
bread, then divide the beans between the 4 slices. Garnish with the red onion
and a few basil leaves and eat at once.

Chicken & spinach empanadas

Makes 8

Filling
300g frozen whole leaf spinach,
    defrosted
1 tbsp olive oil
1 red onion, finely chopped
½ green pepper, finely diced
2 garlic cloves, finely chopped
1 large tomato, diced
250g cooked chicken, diced
zest and juice of 1 lemon
1 tsp ground allspice
½ tsp ground cinnamon
small bunch of parsley, finely
    chopped
leaves from 3 large mint sprigs,
    finely chopped
25g capers
salt and black pepper

Pastry
250g plain flour, plus extra
    for dusting
½ tsp baking powder
pinch of salt
50ml olive oil, plus extra
    for brushing
50ml white wine or fino sherry

Empanadas are the Spanish version of a pasty and hugely popular in South America. Like a pasty, they are the perfect portable snack and great for a high tea, a picnic or just when you fancy a little something. These have a really lovely flavourful filling.

First make the pastry. Put the flour and baking powder in a bowl and add a good pinch of salt. Drizzle in the olive oil and white wine or fino sherry and mix briefly. Add just enough water to bind it all together – 2–3 tablespoons at most – and make a firm, pliable dough. Knead the dough until smooth, then cover it and leave it for half an hour.

To make the filling, squeeze any liquid out of the spinach and roughly chop. Leave the spinach in a sieve to drain. Heat the olive oil in a wide frying or sauté pan, add the red onion and green pepper and sauté for several minutes until the onion is translucent. Add all the remaining ingredients, including the spinach, and cook for a few minutes until the mixture is well combined and lightly cooked. Leave to cool.

To assemble the empanadas, divide the dough into 8 evenly sized pieces and knead each piece into a ball. Roll out each ball into a disc measuring about 16cm in diameter. Put an eighth of the filling on one half of a disc. Wet the edges, then fold them over and crimp them together. The dough should be very forgiving and will stretch well. Repeat to make the remaining empanadas.

Preheat the oven to 200°C/Fan 180°C/Gas 6. Arrange the empanadas on a large baking tray and brush them with oil. Bake in the oven for 20–25 minutes until golden brown with a piping hot filling.

Savoury potato waffles

Serves 4

600g potatoes in their skins
(or 550g leftover mash)
85g plain flour
15g cornflour
1 tsp baking powder
100g buttermilk
2 tsp wholegrain mustard
leaves from a thyme sprig
2 eggs, separated
125g strong cheese, such as
mature Cheddar, grated
butter, for greasing
salt and black pepper

To serve
bacon, fried or poached eggs
or whatever you fancy

Waffles are just the job for high tea – or for brunch or lunch or any time. We like these savoury waffles topped with a fried or poached egg or served American style with a drizzle of maple syrup and bacon. Some roast tomatoes and garlicky soured cream are also really good accompaniments. Try these ideas or experiment – this is a great waffle mix and the waffles even taste good when cold.

Put the potatoes in a steamer and set them over simmering water. Cook for 25–30 minutes until tender. When they are cool enough to handle, remove the skins and push the potatoes through a ricer. Beat in the butter until it has melted and season with salt and pepper, then leave the potato to cool to room temperature. If you use leftover mash, be sure to heat it through before adding the butter.

Mix the flour, cornflour and baking powder together and season with salt. Beat the buttermilk, mustard, thyme and egg yolks into the potatoes, then fold in the flour mixture and the cheese.

Beat the egg whites to the stiff peaks stage, then fold them into the mash, a heaped tablespoon at a time. The batter will loosen up a bit but will still be quite firm, which is fine.

Heat a waffle maker and brush it with plenty of butter, top and bottom. Spoon the waffle batter on to the maker, spreading it as evenly as possible with a palette knife. Do not over fill, as the waffles will rise – just over the tips of the points is enough. Cook until the waffles are crisp and brown on the outside and don't try to lift them until they come away from the maker cleanly – this can take up to 10 minutes.

Keep the waffles warm while you make the rest, adding plenty of butter between each batch. There should be enough batter for 4 rounds.

Rock buns

Makes 8

250g self-raising flour
1 tsp baking powder
pinch of salt
125g butter, chilled and diced
100g light brown soft sugar
100g raisins or sultanas
50g glacé cherries
1 egg, beaten
50ml milk or buttermilk

I don't ever bake a rock bun without thinking of the tiny house in Team Valley, near Gateshead, where my Auntie Hilda and Uncle George lived. The smell of Auntie Hilda's home baking was something to savour and her rock buns were second to none. Uncle George always insisted on taking the top off his bun and filling it with Auntie Hilda's home-made apricot jam. (Si)

Preheat the oven to 180°C/Fan 160°C/Gas 4.

Put the flour in a bowl with the baking powder and a generous pinch of salt. Mix them together briefly, then add the butter and rub it in until the mixture resembles fine breadcrumbs.

Add the sugar, raisins or sultanas and glacé cherries. Whisk the egg and milk or buttermilk together, then stir this into the flour mixture and stir to form a firm but sticky dough.

Line a baking tray with baking parchment. Divide the mixture into 8, form them into rough-looking mounds and place them on the baking tray. The mounds should look craggy, so if you think they look too smooth, rough them up a little with a fork.

Bake the buns in the preheated oven for 15–20 minutes until golden brown – don't worry if they still seem soft, as they will firm up as they cool.

Transfer the rock buns to a rack to cool. Enjoy them warm or cold, as they are or broken up and spread with butter – or jam if you're like Uncle George!

Stout fruit cake

Makes 10–12 slices

200g butter, diced, plus extra
for greasing
250g plain flour
25g cocoa powder
2 tsp mixed spice
2 tsp baking powder
pinch of salt
200g dark brown soft sugar
200ml stout (such as Guinness
West Indies Porter)
700g dried fruit (mix of glacé
cherries, raisins, chopped
prunes, finely chopped
candied orange peel)
zest of 1 orange
3 eggs, beaten

There's nothing like knowing you have a cake like this to come home to and enjoy with a cup of tea after a hard day. We make this cake using the traditional boiled method – boiling up the fruit, butter and sugar with a good measure of stout – so it's very easy and the result is smashing. Keeps well too, if you let it, and it's full of flavour – the cocoa works well with the slight bitterness of the stout.

Preheat the oven to 160°C/Fan 140°C/Gas 3. Butter a deep 20cm cake tin and line it with baking parchment. Tie a double layer of parchment around the outside to protect the cake.

Put the flour, cocoa, mixed spice and baking powder into a bowl with a generous pinch of salt and whisk together.

Put the butter, sugar and stout into a large saucepan. Place the pan over a gentle heat and stir the mixture regularly until the butter and sugar have melted, then add the dried fruit and orange zest. Bring to the boil, then remove the pan from the heat. Leave to cool a little, then beat in the eggs and fold in the dry ingredients.

Scrape the mixture into the tin and bake the cake in the preheated oven for about one hour to an hour and 15 minutes. The cake will be done when a skewer inserted into the middle comes out clean and the cake has shrunk away from the sides of the tin slightly. You can also check the temperature with a cooking thermometer – it should be at least 98°C in the centre.

Leave the cake to cool in the tin, then remove it and wrap it well in baking parchment or foil. Store in an airtight tin. If you can, wait for at least a couple of days before eating, as the texture will improve enormously.

Clifton puffs

Makes 20

1 x 320g pack of puff pastry
1 egg, beaten
caster sugar, for sprinkling

Filling
100g raisins or sultanas
50g currants
50g pitted dates, chopped
50g candied orange peel,
    finely chopped
zest of 1 lemon
2 eating apples, peeled
    and finely diced
50g dark brown soft sugar
75ml brandy or rum
50g ground almonds
50g almonds, finely chopped
a few drops of almond extract
    (optional)
1 tsp ground cinnamon
pinch of salt

Clifton is an area of Bristol and it's said that these light, crisp little pastries were first made to celebrate the opening of the Clifton Suspension Bridge in the 19th century. Whatever the story, the pastries are so good and not hard to make. A perfect addition to your teatime table.

Put the dried fruit, peel, zest and apples in a small saucepan with the sugar. Pour over the alcohol and heat gently, while stirring, until the sugar has dissolved. Cover and leave over a low heat for 5 minutes – most of the liquid should have been absorbed by the dried fruit. Stir in the ground almonds, chopped almonds, almond extract and cinnamon with a generous pinch of salt and leave to cool completely.

Preheat the oven to 200°C/Fan 180°C/Gas 6 and line a large baking tray with baking parchment.

Roll out the pastry to about 32 x 40cm and cut it into 20 squares measuring 8 x 8cm. Put a spoonful of the filling in the centre of a square. Bring the corners of the square into the middle over the filling and pinch them together. Brush the pastry with beaten egg and sprinkle with sugar. Repeat to fill the remaining squares.

Bake the puffs in the oven for 15–20 minutes, turning them once, until they are a rich golden brown. Best served hot or warmed through.

Bostok

Makes 8

Sugar syrup
50g caster sugar
juice of 1 mandarin or clementine
1 tbsp rum (optional)

Frangipane
100g butter, softened
100g caster sugar
zest of 1 mandarin or clementine
pinch of salt
1 egg
100g ground almonds

To assemble
8 slices of brioche or white bread
3–4 tbsp raspberry jam
25g flaked almonds

To serve
250g raspberries
250ml crème fraiche

Sort of a happy marriage between French toast and an almond croissant, this French breakfast treat is just as good at teatime. The jam isn't traditional, but we like it and it gives the bostok a Bakewell vibe. Mouthwateringly good, we reckon.

First make the sugar syrup. Put the sugar into a saucepan, then pour the juice into a measuring jug and make it up to 50ml with water. Add this to the pan. Heat gently, stirring until the sugar has dissolved, then simmer for 2–3 minutes until the mixture looks syrupy. Add the rum, if using, then set aside to cool.

To make the frangipane, beat the butter and sugar together with the zest and a pinch of salt, until soft and fluffy, then beat in the egg and ground almonds.

Preheat the oven to 180°C/Fan 160°C/Gas 5. Arrange the brioche slices on a baking tray lined with baking paper. Brush them with the sugar syrup, making sure you use it all, then brush them with some jam. Divide the frangipane between the slices and spread it evenly with a palette knife. Sprinkle with the flaked almonds.

Bake in the oven for about 15 minutes or until the frangipane has set and is a rich golden brown. The almonds should look lightly toasted. Serve hot or cold with berries and spoonfuls of crème fraiche.

Stem ginger & lemon drizzle cake

Makes about 12 slices

175g butter, softened, plus extra
    for greasing
175g golden caster sugar
2 balls of stem ginger, rinsed,
    dried and very finely chopped
zest of 1 lemon
pinch of salt
3 eggs
225g self-raising flour
3–4 tbsp milk

Topping
juice of 1 lemon
2-3 tbsp ginger syrup
1 ball of stem ginger, rinsed,
    dried and finely chopped
2 tbsp granulated sugar

A good drizzle cake is an all-time favourite and this one combines stem ginger with the traditional lemon to make an extra special teatime treat. Everyone will love this.

Preheat the oven to 180°C/Fan 160°C/Gas 4. Grease a large loaf tin with butter and line it with baking parchment.

Beat the butter and sugar together with the stem ginger, lemon zest and a generous pinch of salt, until soft and fluffy. Add the eggs, one at a time, with a couple of tablespoons of the flour with each addition. Fold in the rest of the flour and just enough milk to give the batter a reluctant dropping consistency.

Scrape the mixture into the prepared tin and put it in the oven. Bake for about 45 minutes until the cake is well risen, springy to the touch and has shrunk away slightly from the sides of the tin. The top may crack a little – but this is normal for this type of cake. Leave the cake in the tin.

Mix the lemon juice, ginger syrup and stem ginger together. Pierce the cake all over with a skewer. Add the granulated sugar to the syrup and pour it all over the cake while it is still warm from the oven. Try to make sure most of the syrup goes on top, rather than down the sides. Rearrange some of the stem ginger as necessary, so it is evenly spread over the cake. Leave the cake in the tin to cool completely, then store it in an airtight container.

Chocolate & fudge cookies

Makes 24

125g plain flour
75g cocoa powder
1 tsp bicarbonate of soda
150g fudge (shop-bought
　　or see p.270), diced
125g unsalted butter, softened
50g granulated sugar
150g light brown soft sugar
1 egg
2 tsp vanilla extract
salt

We all love a bit of fudge and these little beauties contain some chunks of fudge in the mixture, plus some more on the top. If you bake the cookies straight away, they will turn out quite flat but if you prefer a deeper cookie, chill the mixture briefly first. Lovely with a cuppa to brighten up your afternoon.

Preheat the oven to 170°C/Fan 150°C/Gas 3½ and line a couple of baking trays with baking parchment.

Put the flour in a bowl with the cocoa powder, bicarbonate of soda and a generous pinch of salt. Add 100g of the fudge and mix together thoroughly.

Beat the butter and sugars together until very soft and fluffy. Beat in the egg and vanilla extract, then fold in the dry ingredients.

Divide the mixture into 24 balls and arrange them on the baking trays. Space them out well so they don't run into one another. Sprinkle the remaining fudge on top, then add a scant sprinkling of salt.

Bake the cookies in the preheated oven for about 12 minutes until they have spread and have a cracked appearance. They may puff up but this will subside when they have cooled a little. The fudge will also lightly caramelise.

Remove the cookies from the oven and leave them on the baking trays for a few minutes to firm up, then transfer to a cooling rack.

Chocolate eclairs

Makes about 8-12

Choux pastry
115g plain flour
100g butter
2 tsp caster sugar
1 tsp vanilla extract
pinch of salt
3 eggs, well beaten
1 tbsp icing sugar

Filling
300ml double cream
1 tbsp icing sugar
½ tsp vanilla extract

Chocolate glaze
100g dark chocolate
　　(or 50g dark chocolate
　　and 50g milk chocolate)
50g whipping cream
50g butter
25g golden syrup

Possibly everyone's top teatime pleasure, eclairs are a bit of work but so worth it. Just picture yourself biting into that beautiful choux pastry filled with cream and spread with chocolate – as you can see, Andrew, our photographer, couldn't wait!

Preheat the oven to 180°C/Fan 160°C/Gas 4 and line 2 baking trays with baking parchment. Sift the flour on to another piece of baking parchment.

Put the butter, sugar, and vanilla extract in a pan with 225ml of water and a generous pinch of salt. Heat gently until the butter has melted and the sugar has dissolved, then turn up the heat until the mixture is boiling. Remove the pan from the heat.

Pull up the sides of the baking parchment and slide the flour into the butter and sugar mixture. Stir the flour into the wet ingredients to form a thick paste which should come away from the sides of the pan in one solid mass. Put the pan back over a gentle heat and continue stirring with a wooden spoon for 2 or 3 minutes, until the mixture is slightly steaming and leaves a floury residue on the base of the pan.

Leave to cool for a couple of minutes, then beat for a couple of minutes more. You can then transfer the dough to a stand mixer or use electric beaters if you prefer. You will see steam escape from the dough at this point. Keep beating until the steam has subsided.

Gradually work in the eggs, just a couple of tablespoons at a time, until you have a thick glossy dough – it needs to be quite stiff and firm enough for you to draw your finger through it without the sides falling back in. The dough initially breaks up a lot, but eventually it will come together again.

Fit a large star or plain round nozzle into a piping bag and scoop the dough into the bag. If you don't have a nozzle, simply snip off the end of the bag off – the hole should be about 2.5cm wide.

Pipe tiny amounts of the dough under the corners of the baking parchment on the trays to keep the parchment in place. For large eclairs, pipe 8 lines of dough, as evenly as possible, on to the baking trays, making each one about 15cm long. To make sure they don't spread to an oval shape, pipe them slightly wider at each end. To make slightly smaller eclairs, pipe 12 lines of about 10 centimetres long. Wet your fingers and smooth out the ends of the eclairs if peaks have formed. If you haven't used a star nozzle, run a fork along the length of each one.

Dust the eclairs with the icing sugar – this will help them darken and crisp up in the oven. Bake for 25 minutes by which time they should have formed a crust. Use a skewer to poke holes in each end of the eclairs so steam can

escape from their centres, then continue to bake for another 8–10 minutes. Turn the oven off and leave the door ajar. Leave the eclairs in the oven for about half an hour – this will help make sure they are crisp all the way through.

To make the filling, whip the cream until it is stiff, then fold in the icing sugar and vanilla extract. Chill for half an hour.

For the glaze, put the chocolate, cream, butter and golden syrup into a bowl over a saucepan of simmering water. Melt together gently to make a fairly thin ganache.

To fill the eclairs, cut 3 holes in the base of each one. Fill a piping bag with the cream and pipe it into the holes. Squeeze the eclairs lightly – they should feel nicely full. Dip each filled éclair in the chocolate glaze – this gives a much better coverage than trying to spread it – then leave them in the fridge to set. These are best eaten on the same day they are made as the pastry will eventually soften, but they will keep for up to 48 hours.

Baked doughnuts

Makes 12–16

Dough
225ml buttermilk
75g butter, softened and diced
2 eggs, beaten
1 tsp vanilla extract
zest of 1 lemon
500g strong white flour
7g fast-acting dried yeast
50g caster sugar
I tsp salt

Honey butter
125g butter
25g honey
6 cardamom pods, lightly crushed
2 tsp vanilla extract

To coat
150g granulated sugar

Doughnuts are usually deep-fried which is a bit of a fiddle, so we've experimented with baking them in the oven instead and it works brilliantly. Less mess and slightly healthier. We've gone for Scandinavian flavours of cardamom and vanilla which we find very comforting. Enjoy these warm from the oven and you'll feel cosy and happy for the rest of the day.

First make the dough. Put the buttermilk in a saucepan and warm very gently until it's at blood temperature. Remove the pan from the heat and add the butter. When it has melted, beat in the eggs and vanilla extract, followed by the lemon zest. Don't worry if the mixture curdles at this stage – it will still work perfectly.

Put the flour in a bowl and stir in the yeast and caster sugar. Add a teaspoon of salt and mix again. Gradually add the wet ingredients until you have a very shaggy, sticky dough. Knead for about 10 minutes until the dough is smooth and shiny – it will still be slightly tacky and very stretchy. Cover with a damp cloth and leave to prove for at least an hour until doubled in size.

Knock the dough back and turn it out. Divide the dough into 12 or 16 pieces, depending on how large you want your doughnuts, then knead into tight balls. Place them on a couple of baking trays, making sure they are well spaced, then cover them with a damp cloth again and leave to prove for a second time.

While the doughnuts are proving, make the honey butter so it has time to infuse with the cardamom. Put the butter, honey, cardamom pods and vanilla extract in a pan and melt everything together, whisking to combine. Set aside to continue infusing.

Preheat the oven to 160°C/Fan 140°C/Gas 3. When the dough balls have puffed up to twice their size again and they spring back when poked, put them in the oven and bake for 15–20 minutes. Keep an eye on them, as you don't want them to develop too dark a crust. The doughnuts are done when they are a light golden-brown and are faintly hollow sounding. The texture should be soft and springy. Just before you take the doughnuts out of the oven, gently reheat the honey butter and strain it.

Remove the doughnuts from the oven. Brush each one liberally with the honey butter, then sprinkle with sugar, making sure they are completely covered. Place them on a rack to cool. Don't wait too long, though, these are at their best when still just warm.

puddings

Pear & banana crumble

Serves 4

Filling

30g butter, diced, plus extra
for greasing
4 pears (ripe but still firm),
peeled and cut into wedges
zest and juice of 1 lime
2 bananas (not too ripe),
peeled and thickly sliced
30g dark brown soft sugar
½ tsp ground cinnamon
½ tsp ground allspice
pinch of salt

Topping

200g plain flour
½ tsp ground cinnamon
pinch of salt
135g butter, diced
75g caster sugar
50g pecans, finely chopped
(optional)

To serve

custard or cream

Who doesn't love a crumble? They're easy to make and so comforting to eat. For our latest version we've combined bananas and pears with a little hint of lime and spice. The flavours go beautifully together – this is a winner we reckon.

Preheat the oven to 200°C/Fan 180°C/Gas 6.

Generously butter a medium-sized ovenproof dish. Toss the pears in the lime zest and juice, then put them in the dish with the bananas and the diced butter. Mix the sugar with the cinnamon, allspice and a pinch of salt. Sprinkle this over the fruit and toss everything together.

To make the topping, put the flour and cinnamon in a bowl with a pinch of salt and add the butter. Rub the butter into the flour, then stir in the sugar and the pecans, if using. Sprinkle the mixture over the filling.

Place the dish on a baking tray and bake the crumble for about 30 minutes until the topping is golden brown and the filling is bubbling through. Serve piping hot with custard or cream.

Lemon steamed pudding

Serves 4-6

Sauce
50g butter
50g light brown soft sugar
1 lemon, very thinly sliced
(optional)
100g lemon curd

Sponge
175g butter, very soft
175g light brown soft sugar
zest of 1 lemon
pinch of salt
175g self-raising flour
3 eggs, beaten
1 tbsp lemon juice

To serve
clotted or pouring cream

There's no way could we write a book on comfort food without including a steamed pudding and this one is fabulous. It does need to steam for a couple of hours but it's easy to make and well worth your time. We like to line the bowl with little lemon slices which look fab when you turn the pud out, but if you don't want to bother, the pudding will still taste great.

You need a pudding basin with a capacity of about 1–1.2 litres. Mix the 50g of butter and 50g of sugar together to make a paste, then spread it thickly over the inside of the pudding basin. Line the basin with the lemon slices, if using, lining the base first before moving round the sides. Finally, put the lemon curd in the base of the basin. Set aside.

For the sponge, put the butter, sugar and lemon zest in a bowl with a generous pinch of salt and beat until soft and fluffy. This is best done in a stand mixer or with hand-held electric beaters. Fold in the flour and eggs, then add just enough lemon juice to give the mixture a dropping consistency.

Spoon the mixture into the pudding basin and smooth the surface. Cover the basin with a lid or with a pleated layer of foil, secured by string or a couple of elastic bands.

Place an upturned heatproof saucer or a folded tea towel in a large, deep pan and put the pudding basin on top. Add enough just-boiled water to come halfway up the sides of the basin. Cover the pan with a tight-fitting lid and place over a low heat, then leave the pudding to steam over the gently simmering water for about 2½ hours. Keep an eye on the water level and top it up from time to time with boiling water. Check the pudding is done by inserting a skewer into the sponge – it should come out clean.

Remove the basin from the steamer. Carefully run a palette knife around the edge of the pudding, just to make sure it is loose enough to turn out. Cover with a plate and turn upside down, then carefully lever off the basin. You should find that the crust and the lemon slices, if using, are lightly caramelised. Best served with clotted or pouring cream.

Rhubarb & strawberry pie

Serves 4–6

Filling
300g rhubarb, sliced
    into 1cm rounds
500g strawberries, hulled
    and chopped
125g caster sugar
3 tbsp cornflour
pinch of salt
zest of 1 orange

Pastry
200g plain flour, plus extra
    for dusting
100g ground almonds
pinch of salt
150g butter, chilled and diced
1 tbsp icing sugar
1 egg, beaten

Topping
milk
caster sugar

Just the title to this recipe makes your mouth water. Two of our favourite fruits all encased in crispy pastry – what could be better? Their flavours go together perfectly. It's important to strain off most of the macerating syrup so you don't get soggy pastry but it's delicious so don't chuck it out. Enjoy it as a cordial or drizzle it over some pancakes.

First start the filling. Put the rhubarb and strawberries in a bowl and sprinkle over half the sugar. Leave the fruit to macerate for an hour.

To make the pastry, put the flour and ground almonds in a bowl with a pinch of salt and add the butter. Rub in the butter until the mixture resembles breadcrumbs, then stir in the icing sugar and the egg. Mix to form a dough, adding a few drops of water if the mixture is too crumbly.

Dust a work surface with flour, roll out two-thirds of the pastry and use to line a deep pie dish. Chill for half an hour.

Strain the fruit, reserving the syrup. Mix the rest of the caster sugar with 2 tablespoons of the syrup, the cornflour and a pinch of salt. Toss the fruit with this mixture and the orange zest, then pile it all into the pie dish, spreading the mixture as evenly as possible. Roll out the remaining pastry and use it to cover the pie. Trim and crimp the edges together, then chill the pie for at least another half an hour.

Preheat the oven to 200°C/Fan 180°C/Gas 6 and put a baking tray in the oven to heat up. Brush the pie with milk and sprinkle evenly with sugar, then cut a couple of slits in the top. Put the pie dish on the baking tray and bake for 40–45 minutes until the crust is golden and the filling is bubbling. Leave the pie to stand for at least 10 minutes before serving.

Irish coffee cheesecake

Serves 6–8

Base
50g butter, melted, plus extra
    butter for greasing
125g biscuits, crushed
50g dark chocolate, cut into
    shards

Filling
125g golden caster sugar
1 tbsp plain flour
pinch of salt
4 tsp instant espresso granules
1 tbsp just-boiled water
1 tsp vanilla extract
3 tbsp Irish whiskey
600g cream cheese, removed from
    the fridge an hour before using
3 eggs
150g soured cream, removed from
    the fridge an hour before using

Topping (optional)
300ml double cream
1 tbsp icing sugar
1 tbsp Irish whiskey
coffee beans, for grating

The idea for this came from Marion, another of my lovely nurses, and it's excellent. If you love an Irish coffee, this cheesecake is for you. The whiskey flavour isn't strong but it's definitely there, so this is a pudding for the grown-ups, not a toddlers' tea party! Do be sure to bring the cream cheese and soured cream up to room temperature, as they will be much easier to work with and your cheesecake will have a better texture. Cheers, Marion and thank you. (Dave)

Butter the sides of a 20cm springform cake tin and line it with baking parchment. Preheat the oven to 160°C/Fan 140°C/Gas 3.

For the base, mix the melted butter and crushed biscuits together and leave them to cool a little. Stir in half the chocolate, then press the mixture into the base of the prepared cake tin. Sprinkle the rest of the chocolate on top. Bake in the oven for 10 minutes, then remove and leave to cool. Turn the oven down to 130°C/Fan 110°C/Gas ½–1.

For the filling, mix the caster sugar and plain flour in a bowl with a generous pinch of salt and set aside. Dissolve the espresso granules in the tablespoon of just-boiled water, then add the vanilla extract and whiskey and set aside.

Put the cream cheese in a large bowl and beat until smooth. Stir in the sugar and flour mixture and beat again until smooth. Beat in the eggs, one at a time, followed by the soured cream. Finally, fold in the coffee and whiskey mixture.

Pour the mixture on top of the biscuit base, then gently shake to make sure it is even. Lift up the tin and drop it a few times to get rid of any air pockets – you might see a few bubbles appear on the surface before they burst.

Bake the cheesecake for 45 minutes or until it's set but still has a slight wobble in the centre. Switch off the oven and leave the cheesecake to cool for 2 hours.

Make sure the cheesecake is at room temperature before transferring it to the fridge for at least another 2 hours, but preferably overnight – this really improves the texture. Run a palette knife around the edge of the cheesecake, then remove it from the tin and place it on a serving plate.

If making the topping, whisk the cream to soft peaks, then stir in the sugar and whiskey. Pile the mixture on top of the cheesecake or serve it on the side. Grate the coffee bean over the cream before serving.

Rice pudding with blackberry compote

Serves 4

150g pudding/short-grain rice
50g light brown soft sugar
2 bay leaves
2 pieces of pared lemon zest
½ cinnamon stick (optional)
900ml whole milk
pinch of salt

Blackberry compote
400g blackberries
juice of ½ lemon
2 tbsp caster sugar
pinch of cinnamon (optional)
2 tsp cornflour

Topping (optional)
75g caster sugar

I know that Stella, my mam, would approve of our new take on a rice pud – she made a great one. This version is as comforting as ever, but we've added a lovely berry compote, plus the option of a caramelised, brûlée-style topping. When blackcurrants are in season they would also make a great compote to use here. (Si)

To make the rice pudding, put the rice, sugar, bay leaves, lemon zest and cinnamon stick, if using, in a large saucepan. Pour over the milk and add a generous pinch of salt.

Bring to the boil, then turn down the heat and leave to simmer gently, stirring regularly to stop the mixture from catching. Continue until the rice is swollen and completely cooked through, and the milk has thickened to a creamy consistency around it. This will take 25–30 minutes.

Put the blackberries in a small saucepan with the lemon juice and caster sugar. Add the cinnamon, if using. Gently heat until the sugar has dissolved and the blackberries have started to release some liquid. Mix the cornflour with a little water to make a thin paste. Stir this into the blackberries until the mixture thickens very slightly into a syrupy sauce.

Put the blackberry compote in a large serving dish or 4 individual pudding bowls. Carefully top with the rice pudding, spooning it around the sides first to make sure a seal is created and the compote doesn't leak through.

Serve as is or, if you want to add a brûlée-style topping, leave the pudding to settle for a few moments, then sprinkle over the sugar as evenly as you can and use a blowtorch to make a caramelised crust.

Cherry dumplings

Makes 16

Dough
500g potatoes, unpeeled
25g butter, diced
1 egg
125g plain flour, plus extra
    for dusting
salt

Filling
24 cherries, pitted and halved
1 tbsp cornflour
1 tbsp caster sugar
½ tsp ground cinnamon

To finish
75g butter
40g fine dried breadcrumbs
75g caster sugar
½ tsp ground cinnamon

To serve
pouring cream or crème fraiche

Known as gomboti, this is a cracking Romanian recipe and Lil, Dave's wife, says it's her favourite pudding. The breadcrumbs for coating the little dumplings should be nice and fine, so if necessary, give them a whizz in the food processor before using.

First make the dough. Put the potatoes in a steamer and cook them over simmering water for 20–25 minutes until tender. Remove the potatoes from the steamer and when they're cool enough to handle, peel them and push them through a ricer into a bowl. Put a tea towel over the bowl and leave the potatoes for 5 minutes – this helps dry them out slightly.

Add the butter, egg, flour and a generous pinch of salt to the potatoes and mix to form a sticky dough, then set aside. Mix the cherries with the cornflour, caster sugar, cinnamon and a pinch of salt, then set aside.

Divide the dough into 16 pieces. Wet your hands with cold water – this is very important as the dough is sticky – and pat each piece of dough into a round. Put 3 cherry halves in the centre of each round and bring the dough up around the sides to enclose the cherries completely and make a fairly round or oval dumpling. Place on a flour-dusted work surface or plate until you have made them all.

Bring a large saucepan of water to the boil. When it is boiling, add half the dumplings which will sink to the bottom. When they have risen to the top, cook them for a further 3 minutes, then drain on kitchen paper. Cook the rest of the dumplings in the same way.

Melt the 75g of butter in a frying pan large enough to hold all the dumplings with plenty of space around them. When the butter is foaming, add the dumplings and fry them until lightly golden on all sides. Sprinkle half the breadcrumbs over the dumplings, then flip them over so they continue to brown with a breadcrumb coating – they should crisp up very well. Sprinkle the top side of the dumplings with the remaining breadcrumbs and flip them so they crisp up and brown on that side too.

Drain the dumplings on kitchen paper again. Mix the sugar and cinnamon together in a bowl. Drop in the dumplings, a few at a time, then toss to coat them. Serve with pouring cream or crème fraiche.

Ginger cake & black cherry trifle

Serves 6–8

Ginger cake
150g plain flour
1 tbsp ground ginger
½ tsp bicarbonate of soda
pinch of salt
100g golden syrup
100g black treacle
60g dark brown soft sugar
75g butter
125ml milk
1 egg, beaten

Trifle
250g pitted sweet cherries,
    fresh or frozen
2 tbsp caster sugar
250g ginger cake
2–3 tbsp black cherry jam
50ml sweet sherry
100g amaretti biscuits
500ml custard (shop-bought
    or see p.271)
250ml double cream
3–4 pieces of stem ginger,
    very finely sliced

A good trifle is the perfect pudding at Christmas or for a celebration at any time of year. The cherries and gingerbread make such a good flavour combination and we know you're going to love this. We've given you a ginger cake recipe, but if you want to cut down on prep time you could always buy a Jamaican ginger cake instead.

First make the cake. Preheat the oven to 170°C/Fan 150°C/Gas 3½. Line a large loaf tin with baking parchment. Put the flour, ginger and bicarbonate of soda into a bowl with a good pinch of salt and whisk together until lump free.

Put the golden syrup, black treacle, sugar and butter in a saucepan and heat gently until melted. Take the pan off the heat, pour the mixture into a bowl and whisk to combine. Add the milk, followed by the egg, then whisk in the flour mixture to form a smooth batter. Pour into the prepared tin and bake for 40–45 minutes until well risen and springy to the touch. Remove from the oven and leave to cool in the tin.

To make the trifle, sprinkle the cherries with the sugar and leave them to stand for half an hour. Thinly slice the cake and spread half the slices with jam. Sandwich them together with the remaining slices. Cut them into fingers and arrange over the base of a trifle bowl.

Strain the cherries – the sugar will have created a syrup around them. Mix this syrup with the sherry and pour half of this liquid over the cake. Top with the cherries, then add the biscuits. Pour over the remaining sherry and syrup.

Pour the custard over the trifle. Whisk the cream to soft peaks and spread it over the custard, making sure it is as evenly spread as possible. Arrange the sliced stem ginger over the top. Chill for at least an hour before serving.

Apple self-saucing pudding

Serves 4–6

butter, for greasing
3 eating apples, peeled and sliced
1 tbsp maple syrup
½ tsp ground cinnamon

Batter
175g self-raising flour
1 tsp ground cinnamon
50g light brown soft sugar
pinch of salt
100g melted butter
50g maple syrup
100ml buttermilk
1 egg

Sauce
100g light brown soft sugar
100g maple syrup
200ml just-boiled water
25g butter

To serve
double cream or custard

Mellow, soothing and delicious – the sauce is created like magic while the pudding cooks. A grand cuddle of a dessert and perfect after your Sunday roast.

Preheat the oven to 180°C/Fan 160°C/Gas 4. Generously butter an ovenproof dish – something fairly shallow with a capacity of about 1.5 litres should be about right. Toss the apples in the maple syrup and cinnamon and arrange them in the base of the dish.

Put the flour, cinnamon and sugar in a bowl with a generous pinch of salt. Whisk together the melted butter, maple syrup, buttermilk and egg in a jug, then pour these wet ingredients into the bowl of dry ingredients. Mix until you have a smooth batter, then scrape this into the dish over the apples and spread it evenly over the top.

For the sauce, sprinkle the sugar over the cake batter. Mix the maple syrup with the just-boiled water and pour it over the top – pour it slowly and steadily over the back of a spoon to keep it even. Dot the butter over the top.

Place the dish on a baking tray and bake the pudding for 40–45 minutes, until the top is golden brown, springy and cake-like, with some of the sauce pushing up round the edges. When you cut into it the apples should be sitting in a light, caramelly sauce. Serve with double cream or custard.

Coconut & tropical fruit pavlova

Serves 6

Meringue
35g desiccated coconut
4 egg whites, at room
    temperature
200g golden caster sugar
½ tsp white wine or cider vinegar
a few drops of coconut essence
    or extract (optional)

Fruit
2–3 mangoes, peeled and sliced
zest and juice of ½ lime, plus
    extra zest to garnish
1–2 tsp rum (optional)
3 passion fruits

Cream
300ml whipping cream
2 tbsp icing sugar
zest and juice of ½ lime
a few drops of coconut essence
    or extract (optional)

We've eaten more than our fair share of pavlovas and have come up with lots of variations, but we're extra happy with this recipe. Coconut, mango and passion fruit give it a truly tropical taste which we certainly find comforting and hugely delicious. Don't overdo the coconut essence or extract – it can be strong.

Preheat the oven to 150°C/Fan 130°C/Gas 2. Take a piece of baking parchment and draw a 24cm circle on it. Place the parchment on a baking tray.

Toast the coconut in a dry frying pan until it's very aromatic and light golden brown in colour. Remove the pan from the heat and spread the coconut over a plate to cool. Blitz it in a small food processor or a clean spice grinder to make fairly fine crumbs, then set aside.

Whisk the egg whites to the dry, stiff peak stage, then gradually add the sugar, a tablespoon at a time, until the mixture is smooth and glossy looking. Add the vinegar and a few drops of coconut extract or essence, if using – be very sparing as it is easy to overdo it. Fold in the toasted coconut.

Arrange the meringue mixture over the round marked out on the baking parchment – build up the sides a little and create peaks with a palette knife. Put the meringue in the oven and immediately turn the oven down to 130°C/Fan 110°C/Gas 1 and bake it for an hour, until it's crisp and golden. Turn the oven off and leave the meringue in the oven to cool completely. Remove the meringue from the oven and put it on a serving plate.

Whisk the cream to soft peaks, then fold in the icing sugar, lime zest and juice and coconut essence or extract, if using. Pile the cream on top of the meringue. Gently toss the mango slices in the lime zest and juice and rum, if using. Arrange the fruit on top of the cream, then scoop out the flesh of the passion fruits and pour over the top. Finish with a little more lime zest.

Chocolate mousse

Serves 4

150g dark chocolate, broken up
1 tsp vanilla extract
zest of ½ orange or 1 clementine
  (optional)
4 eggs, separated
50g icing sugar, sifted, plus 1 tbsp
100ml whipping cream
200g raspberries
2 tbsp framboise/raspberry
  liqueur (optional)

To serve (optional)
crème fraiche
orange zest, for sprinkling

There's a lovely chocolate-orange vibe to this mousse which we really enjoy and it makes this dessert a little bit special. We like the addition of raspberries and raspberry liqueur but feel free to use mandarin segments and orange liqueur if you prefer.

Put the chocolate in a heatproof bowl and set it over a saucepan of simmering water; the bottom of the bowl shouldn't touch the water. When the chocolate has melted, whisk in the vanilla extract and the citrus zest, if using.

Remove the bowl from the heat and leave the chocolate to cool slightly. Beat in the egg yolks, one at a time, followed by the 50g of icing sugar. Don't worry if the mixture seems grainy as you beat in the eggs – it will soon smooth out as you add the sugar.

Lightly whip the cream to the soft peak stage, then fold it through the chocolate mixture – this will help loosen up the mixture before you start adding the egg whites.

Whisk the egg whites until they form stiff peaks. Using a metal spoon, add a couple of tablespoons of the egg whites to the chocolate mixture, then fold them in until completely combined. Fold in the rest of the egg whites until fully incorporated with no streaks. Do this as gently as possible so you don't knock the air out of the whites.

Sprinkle the raspberries with the tablespoon of icing sugar and crush a few very lightly. Drizzle the raspberries with the framboise or raspberry liqueur, if using, and then divide them between 4 serving dishes. Divide the chocolate mousse between the dishes, then leave in the fridge for several hours to set.

Serve as is or top with crème fraiche and sprinkle with orange zest.

Knickerbocker glory

Serves 4

Bananas
4 bananas
juice of ½ lime
150g chocolate, broken up
100g roasted nuts, chopped

Strawberry sauce
200g strawberries, hulled
squeeze of lemon juice
2 tbsp icing sugar

Cream (or use squirty cream)
200ml whipping cream
1 tbsp icing sugar
½ tsp vanilla extract

To assemble
4 cocktail cherries
4 scoops of vanilla ice cream
250g fresh fruit (such as
    strawberries and blueberries)
4 scoops of chocolate ice cream
4 scoops of strawberry ice cream
4 chocolate flakes (optional)
sprinkles or chopped nuts

Who can ever say no to a knickerbocker glory? They are every child's – and Hairy Biker's – dream, and something we used to enjoy at Si's favourite ice cream parlour at Whitley Bay. We've used a mix of different flavours of ice cream here but choose whatever your favourites are – the brownie or cookie dough ones work well too. Do try the frozen bananas as they add a nice bit of extra texture to the feast.

First prepare the bananas. Peel the bananas and toss them in the lime juice. Line a small baking tray with baking paper and put the bananas on top. Put them in the freezer for at least 45 minutes until hard.

Melt the chocolate in a bowl over a pan of simmering water. Sprinkle the nuts over a shallow bowl or plate. Dip the bananas in the melted chocolate, then drop them on to the nuts. Flip them over to coat them completely before the chocolate has a chance to set. Put the coated bananas back on the baking tray and place them in the freezer for at least an hour.

To make the strawberry sauce, blitz the strawberries with the lemon juice and icing sugar until smooth. Set aside.

If using whipping cream, whisk the cream until it forms soft peaks, then stir in the icing sugar and vanilla extract.

To assemble, remove the bananas from the freezer and chop them roughly. If you've left them in the freezer for longer than an hour, they will need 10–15 minutes in the fridge or at room temperature to soften enough for chopping. Some of the chocolate/nut coating will crumble and break off, but this can all be added to the glasses and just provides more texture.

Take 4 tall ice cream sundae glasses and put a cherry in the base of each. Add a scoop of vanilla ice cream to each glass, followed by a drizzle of strawberry sauce, then divide half the fruit and half the chopped bananas between the glasses. Add the chocolate ice cream, followed by more strawberry sauce, the remaining fruit and chopped bananas, and the strawberry ice cream.

Top with whipped or squirty cream and drizzle with the last of the strawberry sauce. Add the chocolate flakes and garnish with some sprinkles or chopped nuts. Devour immediately!

Chocolate & peanut tart

Serves 8

Peanut brittle (optional)
200g white caster sugar
100g unsalted roasted peanuts,
    lightly broken up
pinch of salt

Biscuit base
200g biscuits or cookies
50g butter
50g crunchy peanut butter

Peanut filling
300g dulce de leche
½ tsp vanilla extract
100g peanut butter

Chocolate ganache
200g chocolate, broken up
200ml double cream
1 tsp vanilla extract

If you like chocolate, peanut butter and that amazing stuff called dulce de leche – and who doesn't? – this one's for you. It's easy to make too, just a bit of melting, chilling and mixing and no need to put the oven on.

First make the peanut brittle, if using. Line a baking tray with baking parchment. Put the sugar in a wide saucepan and shake the pan so the sugar coats the base in an even layer. Place the pan over a medium heat and leave until the sugar has melted. After a few minutes, it will turn a deep golden brown. If you find the sugar is melting unevenly around the edges, move the pan around on the heat source to compensate, but don't stir the sugar. Add the peanuts and give the pan a good shake to coat them, then add a pinch of salt. Pour the mixture on to the prepared baking tray and leave to set.

For the biscuit base, line a 20cm round baking tin with baking parchment. Whizz the biscuits in a food processor to form fine crumbs or put them in a bag and bash them with a rolling pin or mallet. Melt the butter and peanut butter together in a saucepan, then remove the pan from the heat. Stir in the biscuit crumbs and then press the mixture into the base of the tin. Chill for at least half an hour.

For the peanut filling, whisk the dulce de leche, vanilla extract and peanut butter together. Spread this over the biscuit base and chill while you make the chocolate ganache.

For the ganache, put the chocolate into a heatproof bowl and place it over a pan of simmering water. When the chocolate has melted, remove the bowl from the heat and whisk in the cream and vanilla extract. Leave to cool, whisking regularly. When the mixture is close to room temperature and thickened, spoon it in a thin layer on top of the peanut filling and smooth it over with a palette knife.

Leave the tart in the fridge for several hours until completely set. Serve as is or, if you've made the peanut brittle, break that up and use it to decorate the top of the tart.

Gooseberry fool

Serves 4

500g gooseberries, topped
    and tailed
75–100g caster sugar
squeeze of lemon juice
300ml double cream
250ml Greek yoghurt
2 tbsp icing sugar
2 tbsp elderflower cordial
    or dessert wine

Gooseberries are only around for a short season but they're well worth enjoying when you can find them in the shops – or if you're lucky enough to have a gooseberry bush. This classic dessert smacks of summer to us and reminds us of times spent at the kitchen table as kids, topping and tailing the fruit. Quite how much sugar you add depends on your gooseberries and how sour or sweet they are, so taste and experiment. Old-fashioned, but fabulous.

Put the gooseberries in a saucepan with the sugar, a squeeze of lemon juice and a splash of water. Heat gently, while stirring, until the sugar has dissolved, then turn up the heat slightly and cook until the gooseberries burst. Remove the pan from the heat and beat the gooseberries to a purée – push the purée through a sieve if you want to remove the seeds. Leave to cool.

Whisk the double cream to the soft peaks stage. Beat the yoghurt with the icing sugar, then fold it into the cream. Stir in the cordial or wine, then taste and add a little more if you like.

Stir the cream and yoghurt mixture through the gooseberry purée, making sure to create a ripple effect rather than completely combining. Chill the fool until you are ready to eat.

Peach cobbler

Serves 4–6

Filling
butter, for greasing
6 peaches, cut into wedges
    (peel them if you like)
25g dark brown soft sugar
1 tsp vanilla extract
1 tbsp cornflour
pinch of salt

Topping
225g self-raising flour
1 tsp baking powder
salt
100g chilled butter, diced
75g light brown soft sugar
100ml buttermilk
1 egg
1 tsp vanilla extract

We love a cobbler and this peach version is a keeper, a taste of the Deep South. We've kept it really simple – there's just a little touch of vanilla that goes beautifully with the peaches, and we use dark sugar on the peaches to give a lovely butterscotchy flavour. The peaches should be ripe but not too soft and you can peel them or not, as you prefer.

Preheat the oven to 180°C/Fan 160°C/Gas 4. Butter an oval, ovenproof dish and put the peaches in the base. Put the sugar in a small bowl and sprinkle over the vanilla extract. Rub the sugar between your fingers to distribute the vanilla evenly and to break up any lumps, then add the cornflour and a pinch of salt. Mix well, then sprinkle the mixture over the peaches and stir so they are nicely coated.

Put the flour and baking powder in a bowl with a generous pinch of salt and add the butter. Rub the butter into the flour until it resembles fine breadcrumbs, then stir in the sugar. Whisk the buttermilk, egg and vanilla extract together, then mix with the dry ingredients until well combined – the mixture will be soft and sticky, slightly looser in texture than dumplings.

Take heaped spoonfuls of the dough and arrange them over the peaches. Bake in the preheated oven for 30–35 minutes until the crust is well risen and lightly browned, and the juice from the peaches is bubbling through. Delicious hot, warm or cold.

Caramelised apple cheesecake

Serves 6

Base
175g biscuits
50g dried apples, very finely
      chopped
50g pecans, very finely chopped
½ tsp ground cinnamon
100g butter

Cream cheese filling
200g ricotta, at room
      temperature
300g cream cheese, at room
      temperature
½ tsp ground cinnamon
50g icing sugar
pinch of salt
50g soured cream
½ tsp vanilla extract

Caramelised apples
3 or 4 apples, peeled, cored
      and cut into wedges
juice of ½ lemon
1 tsp ground cinnamon
½ tsp ground allspice
¼ tsp ground cloves
200g caster sugar (make sure
      it's cane sugar)
50g butter
pinch of salt
25ml calvados, brandy or whisky
100ml double cream

Some people like a baked cheesecake (see page 220), others prefer the fridge-set sort, so we have both in this book, as they're super-comforting desserts. Our advice is to try making both – they are epic, and we can't choose between them.

Line a deep 20cm diameter cake tin – preferably a loose-bottomed springform tin – with baking parchment. Put the biscuits in a food processor and blitz them to form fine crumbs. Add the dried apples and pecans and process again until they are well combined with the biscuits, then stir in the cinnamon. Melt the butter in a saucepan, then take the pan off the heat, add the biscuit mixture and mix thoroughly. Press the mixture into the base of the tin and chill for at least half an hour.

To make the filling, put the ricotta and cream cheese in a bowl and whisk lightly to combine. Beat in the cinnamon and sugar, along with a pinch of salt. Finally, add the soured cream and vanilla extract and beat briefly to combine. Spoon the filling over the base in the tin, smoothing it over with a palette knife. Transfer the cheesecake to the fridge and leave to chill.

To make the topping, put the apples in a bowl and toss them in the lemon juice, then the spices. Set aside. Put the 200g of sugar in a wide-based pan. Stir in 50ml of water so the sugar has the consistency of wet sand, then place the pan over a medium-high heat until the sugar caramelises. Don't be tempted to move the sugar around with a spoon – just move the pan to avoid a particular patch from burning if it's cooking unevenly.

When the sugar has caramelised, add the butter. It will bubble furiously at first but just wait for it to subside, then whisk it into the sugar. Add a generous pinch of salt. Drain the apples and add them to the pan in a single layer. Leave them to cook over a low-medium heat for a few minutes on each side. The sauce will continue to darken and reduce around them. When the apples are knife tender, but not collapsing, remove them from the pan with a slotted spoon and set aside on a lined baking tray to cool.

Add the alcohol to the caramel sauce in the pan and let it bubble for a minute or so, then stir in the cream. There's a chance the mixture might seize at this point but keep stirring or whisking and it will soon turn into a smooth sauce. Remove from the heat and leave to cool.

Remove the cheesecake from its tin. Arrange the apples over the top and drizzle with the caramel sauce. Chill until ready to serve.

sides
& basics

Buttery mash

Serves 6

1kg floury potatoes, such as King
    Edwards or Maris Pipers
75ml single cream or milk
50g butter
salt and black pepper

Peel the potatoes and cut them into chunks. Try to make sure the pieces are roughly the same size, so they cook evenly.

Put the potatoes in a pan of salted water and bring to the boil. Once the water is boiling, turn down the heat and simmer the potatoes for about 20 minutes or until soft. Warm the cream or milk in a separate pan and melt the butter. It really is worth doing this, as it will help keep the mash hot for longer.

When the potatoes are cooked, drain them well and tip them back into the pan. Mash them thoroughly, giving them a really good pummelling. Add the warm cream or milk and the butter and mix well, then season to taste. Serve at once.

Dauphinoise potatoes

Serves 4-6

1 garlic clove, cut in half
25g butter
1kg salad/waxy potatoes, such
    as Charlottes, thinly sliced
300ml double cream
400ml whole milk
1 tsp plain flour
grating of nutmeg (optional)
salt and black pepper

Preheat the oven to 180°C/Fan 160°C/Gas 4.

Rub a shallow gratin dish with the cut sides of the garlic, then take a small knob of the butter and rub this around the dish as well.

Rinse the potatoes to get rid of excess starch, then dry them as thoroughly as you can. Layer them in the gratin dish, seasoning them with salt and black pepper as you go.

Put the double cream and milk in a jug and whisk in the flour – this helps to stop the cream curdling. Pour the mixture over the potatoes, then dot the remaining butter on top. Grate over some nutmeg, if using.

Bake in the preheated oven for an hour, then turn the heat up to 220°C/Fan 200°C/Gas 7 and bake for another 10 minutes or until the top layer of potatoes has turned a crisp golden-brown.

Roast potatoes

Serves 4-6

1.5kg potatoes, such as Maris
    Pipers
100g goose or duck fat
2 tbsp semolina
salt and black pepper

Peel the potatoes and cut them into large chunks. Put the potatoes in a pan of cold, salted water, bring the water to the boil and boil for about 5 minutes. Drain well in a colander, then tip the potatoes back into the pan and shake them to scuff up the surfaces. This helps to make lovely crispy roasties.

Meanwhile, preheat the oven to 200–220°C/Fan 180–200°C/Gas 6–7. Put the goose or duck fat in a roasting tin and place it in the oven to heat up. It must be really good and hot. Sprinkle the semolina over the potatoes and carefully tip them into the sizzling fat. Season well, then roast the potatoes for 45–50 minutes until golden and crisp. Serve at once. Great with the skirlie chicken on page 158.

Triple-cooked chips

Serves 4

1kg potatoes, preferably Maris
    Pipers
groundnut or sunflower oil, for
    deep-frying
salt

Peel the potatoes and cut them into thick batons, about 1.5 x 1.5 x 6cm in size. Run them under cold water to remove as much starch as possible, then put them in a large pan.

Cover the chips with cold water and slowly bring it to the boil. Simmer gently for 20–25 minutes, until the potatoes are tender when tested with the point of a knife and you can see lines and cracks start to appear. Using a slotted spoon, remove the chips very carefully from the pan and drain them on some kitchen paper. Pat them dry with more kitchen paper.

Half-fill a deep-fat fryer or large saucepan with oil and heat to 130°C. Be very careful when deep-frying and never leave the pan unattended. Fry the chips in a couple of batches, until they have developed a crust but not taken on any colour. This will take about 5 minutes. Remove each batch when it's ready and set aside.

Now heat the oil to 180°C. Put the chips back in the pan, again in a couple of batches, and fry them for 1–2 minutes until they're very crisp and deep golden-brown in colour. Drain the chips on kitchen paper, then sprinkle them with salt and serve immediately.

By the way, if you happen to have some beef dripping handy you can use that for frying your chips – it gives extra-special flavour. You'll need about 1.5kg.

Cauliflower cheese

Serves 4

1 large cauliflower
25g butter
2 tbsp plain flour
250ml whole milk
½ tsp English mustard powder
200g Gruyère cheese, grated
grating of nutmeg
50g Parmesan cheese, grated
salt and black pepper

Trim the cauliflower and break it into florets. Bring a big pan of water to the boil, add the cauliflower florets and boil them for about 10 minutes until just tender. Drain and set aside. Preheat the oven to 180°C/Fan 160°C/Gas 4.

Melt the butter in a small saucepan and beat in the flour. Add the milk, stirring all the time, to make a thick white sauce. Add the mustard powder and grated Gruyère while stirring, then season with salt and black pepper.

Put the cauliflower florets in an ovenproof dish, pour in the cheesy sauce and sprinkle with a grating of nutmeg. Sprinkle the grated Parmesan on top. Place in the preheated oven and bake for about 15 minutes or until the sauce is bubbling and the top is golden.

Rice & peas

Serves 4

1 tbsp coconut or vegetable oil
1 onion, finely chopped
200g basmati rice, well rinsed
　　and drained
200ml coconut milk
400g can of red kidney beans,
　　black beans or gungo peas
1 thyme sprig
¼ tsp ground allspice
salt and black pepper

Warm the oil in a large saucepan over a medium heat, then add the onion. Cook gently for a minute or so, then stir in the rice. Pour in the coconut milk and 400ml of water, then add the beans, thyme and allspice. Season with salt and pepper.

Bring to the boil, then turn down the heat to a simmer and cover the pan with a lid. Leave the rice and beans to cook for 15–20 minutes until all the liquid has been absorbed. Take the pan off the heat and leave it to stand, covered, for 5 minutes, before serving. Great with the brisket on page 136.

Onion gravy

Serves 4

50g butter
3 onions, finely sliced
1 garlic clove, finely chopped
    (optional)
1 tsp sugar
100ml red wine
large thyme sprig
1 bay leaf
600ml well-flavoured beef stock
dash of Worcestershire sauce
    (optional)
sea salt and black pepper

To thicken (optional)
1 tbsp flour
15g butter, softened

Melt the butter in a wide saucepan or a lidded sauté pan and add the onions. Sauté them gently until they are soft and translucent, then add the garlic, if using, and cook for a few more minutes. Stir in the sugar and turn up the heat. Continue to cook, stirring regularly, until the onions are a rich brown colour and nicely caramelised.

Pour in the red wine, add the herbs and bring to the boil. Allow the wine to reduce down by at least two-thirds, then pour in the stock. Add the Worcestershire sauce, if using, and season with salt and pepper. Bring to the boil, then turn down the heat, cover and leave to simmer for 10 minutes.

The gravy can be served like this or you can thicken it, if you prefer. To do this, mash the flour and butter together, then whisk a teaspoon at a time into the simmering gravy. Keep whisking until the mixture has dissolved and the gravy is the consistency you want.

Duck confit

Serves 4

25g sea salt
leaves from 1 large thyme sprig
2 dried bay leaves, crumbled
1 tsp allspice berries, lightly
     crushed
1 tsp black peppercorns, lightly
     crushed
2 garlic cloves, crushed or grated
4 duck legs
500g duck or goose fat

You only need 2 duck legs for the shepherd's pie recipe on page 162, but it's well worth making more while you're at it and they keep very well.

Mix the salt, herbs, spices and garlic together and rub this mixture over the duck legs. Cover and leave them in the fridge overnight.

Preheat the oven to 150°C/Fan 130°C/Gas 2.

Wipe the duck legs clean and place them in a casserole dish – they should be quite a snug fit. Add the duck or goose fat – it won't quite cover the legs initially but should do by the end of the cooking process. Cover and put the dish in the oven for 2½–3 hours, checking at intervals, until the duck is tender and falling off the bone.

Transfer the duck and fat to a sterilised jar. Push the legs down below the fat – if they are completely covered they will keep for weeks. Allow to cool – the fat will set in this time – before transferring to the fridge.

Korma spice mix

Makes 1 jar

1 tbsp ground cinnamon
1 tbsp ground cardamom
1 tbsp ground coriander
1 tbsp ground turmeric
1½ tsp ground white pepper
½ tsp ground mace
½ tsp ground cloves

Mix all the spices together and store in an airtight jar. This makes more than you need for the korma recipe on page 128, but keeps well.

Vietnamese curry paste

Makes a bowlful

4 garlic cloves, roughly chopped
2 shallots, roughly chopped
15g root ginger, sliced
2 lemon grass stalks, white centre
    only, roughly chopped
1 red chilli, roughly chopped
1 tsp ground turmeric
1 tsp curry powder
½ tsp ground cinnamon
2 tsp light brown soft sugar
    or palm sugar

Put all the ingredients into a small food processor and blitz to form a smooth paste, pushing everything down regularly and adding water if necessary. Use this paste for the coconut noodle soup on page 28 and the Vietnamese fish curry on page 122.

Quick preserved lemons

Makes 1 jar

2 large unwaxed lemons
½ tsp salt

We like this quick version of preserved lemons, as you get a savoury lemon syrup that can be used in all kinds of sauces and salad dressings.

Pare the zest off the lemons with a vegetable peeler. Check the zest and trim off any thick pieces of pith. Juice the lemons and put the juice in a small saucepan with the pared zest and the salt.

Bring to the boil, then turn down the heat, cover the pan and simmer for about 10 minutes, until the zest is soft and the juice has thickened to a syrupy consistency.

Tip the mixture into a small, sterilised jar and leave to cool. It will keep in the fridge indefinitely. This recipe also works well with limes or Seville oranges.

Chilli relish

Makes 1 jar

1 tbsp olive oil
1 red onion, finely chopped
1 red pepper (we like the long
    peppers as they are thinner
    fleshed), finely diced
1 hot chilli pepper, finely diced
3 garlic cloves, finely diced
400g can of tomatoes or fresh
    equivalent
2 tbsp light brown soft sugar
2 tbsp red wine vinegar
zest and juice of ½ lemon
chilli flakes (optional)
salt and black pepper

Heat the olive oil in a sauté pan. Add the red onion, red pepper and chilli pepper, then sauté until the onion is soft and translucent. Add the garlic and cook for another 2–3 minutes.

Add the tomatoes, sugar and red wine vinegar with 100ml of water. Season with plenty of salt and pepper, then stir until the sugar has dissolved. Bring to the boil, then turn the heat down and simmer until the mixture has reduced down to a thick, jammy sauce. Stir regularly to make sure it doesn't catch on the bottom of the pan. Stir in the lemon zest and juice and cook for a few more minutes.

Taste the relish and add chilli flakes if you need more of a kick. Leave to cool, then spoon it into a sterilised jar and store in the fridge for up to a week. Perfect with the Glamorgan sausage rolls on page 184.

Tomato sauce

Makes about 1 litre

6 tbsp olive oil
2 onions, very finely sliced
6 garlic cloves, finely chopped
250ml red wine
4 x 400g cans of chopped
    tomatoes, or 1.5kg plum
    tomatoes, peeled and chopped
2 tsp dried oregano
1 tsp fresh thyme leaves
2 bay leaves
pinch of sugar (optional)
salt and black pepper

Great to have some of this in the fridge or freezer for a quick and comforting pasta supper.

Heat the olive oil in a large saucepan and add the onions. Sauté them very gently until soft – this will take at least 15 minutes.

Add the garlic and cook for another 3–4 minutes over a very gentle heat, then pour in the red wine. Boil until the wine is reduced by at least half, add the tomatoes and herbs, then season with salt and pepper.

Bring the sauce to the boil, then turn down the heat, cover the pan and simmer for an hour. At this point, taste the sauce and if it seems too acidic, add a generous pinch of sugar. Continue to simmer, uncovered, for about another 30 minutes until well reduced. Use immediately or leave to cool, then store in the fridge or freezer.

Tartare sauce

Serves 4

1 egg yolk
pinch of salt
1 tsp Dijon mustard
250ml neutral-tasting oil
    (sunflower or groundnut)
zest of 1 lime
4 tbsp cornichons, finely chopped
3 tbsp capers, finely chopped
a few chives, snipped
a few tarragon leaves
a few basil leaves
a squeeze of lime juice
1 tsp sriracha sauce (optional)

Put the egg yolk in a bowl or food processor with a generous pinch of salt and the mustard. Whisk or pulse briefly, then very gradually start adding the oil.

When the mixture has emulsified, start adding the oil in a steady, slightly faster stream until it is all incorporated and you have a thick mayonnaise. Stir through the remaining ingredients and taste for seasoning.

Perfect with the prawn and fish balls on page 58 or with any grilled fish.

Gyoza wrappers

Makes 24

75g strong white flour
75g plain flour, plus extra
    for dusting
75ml just-boiled water
½ tsp salt

These are ideal for the potstickers on page 156. Put both flours into a bowl. Mix the just-boiled water with the salt, then add this to the flour, mixing it in with a knife. The mixture will seem very floury to start with but keep going and it will come together. Don't be tempted to add more water.

Cover the bowl with a damp cloth and leave for 10 minutes, then remove the dough and knead until it is smooth and elastic. Cover the dough again and leave it to prove somewhere warm for an hour.

Cut the dough into 2 equal pieces and dust a work surface with flour. Roll the dough out as thinly as you can. It will be resistant to start with, but you will eventually end up with a round of about 35cm in diameter and with a thickness of less than 1mm.

Cut the dough into rounds using a 9cm cutter, then repeat with the other piece of dough. Knead the offcuts together and roll again. You should get at least 24 discs. If you want to stack the discs together, dust with flour between each one.

Bao buns

Makes 12 small or 8 medium bao buns

250g plain flour
1 tsp baking powder
1 tsp fast-acting dried yeast
1 tbsp caster sugar
1 tsp salt
100ml warm water
50ml milk
1 tbsp vegetable oil

You can buy bao buns for the Szechuan lamb recipe on page 172, but home-made are even better. Cut out 8–12 rounds of baking parchment or flatten out some paper muffin cases.

Put the flour in a large bowl or in the bowl of a stand mixer and add the baking powder, yeast and sugar. Mix briefly, then add the salt. Gradually work in the water and milk until you have a fairly stiff dough. Leave it to rest for 10 minutes, then knead until the dough is very smooth.

Cover the dough with cling film or a damp cloth and leave it somewhere warm until it has doubled in size – this will probably take at least an hour. Divide the dough into 8 or 12 pieces and roll each portion into a ball. Roll each ball into a thin oval and brush with oil. Place a chopstick down the middle and fold the dough in half, then pull the chopstick out and place the buns on to a piece of parchment or flattened muffin case. Repeat with the remaining balls of dough, then leave them to double in size again.

Prepare a steamer. When the water is boiling, add the buns to the steamer basket, still on their parchment – best to do this in 2–3 batches, depending on the size of the steamer. It's OK for the buns to touch, but make sure they aren't squashed together. Steam for 8–10 minutes until cooked through and puffed up. Fill as in the recipe on page 172.

Garlic & coriander naan breads

Makes 8

500g strong white bread flour,
    plus extra for dusting
7g fast-acting dried yeast
2 tsp caster sugar
2 tsp mustard seeds
2 tsp garlic powder
3 tbsp coriander stems, finely
    chopped
1½ tsp salt
150g plain yoghurt
200ml tepid water

Garlic & coriander butter

100g butter
4 garlic cloves, crushed or grated
leaves from a small bunch of
    coriander, finely chopped

Put the flour in a bowl and add the yeast and sugar. Mix thoroughly, then add the mustard seeds, garlic powder, coriander stems and salt. Mix in the yoghurt, then work in the water to make a soft sticky dough.

Leave the dough to stand for half an hour, then either knead it for 10 minutes using a dough hook on a stand mixer or turn it out on to a lightly floured surface and knead by hand until smooth. If you are finding the dough quite sticky to work with, don't be tempted to add more flour – just wet or lightly oil your hands instead. Put the dough back in the bowl, cover it with a damp cloth and leave it to rise until it has doubled in size.

Divide the dough into 8 pieces and stretch out each piece into a tear-shaped flatbread. Heat a dry frying pan and cook each flatbread for 2–3 minutes on each side, waiting for the dough to be almost cooked through before flipping it– you should get some speckled browning or light charring.

Melt the butter in a small saucepan and add the garlic. Leave it over a low heat for a few minutes, then stir in the coriander.

Reheat each naan in a frying pan, brushing liberally with the garlic and coriander butter, until the naan is soft and piping hot.

Rough puff pastry

Makes about 500g

225g plain flour, plus extra for
    dusting
pinch of salt
225g butter, chilled and diced
125ml iced water

Put the flour in a bowl with a generous pinch of salt. Add the butter and toss it in the flour until it is completely coated. Squash each cube of butter as flat as you can – do not be tempted to do anything else – then stir in the iced water and form the mixture into a dough. Keep the mixing to an absolute minimum as you do not want to break up the butter. Chill the dough for at least half an hour in the fridge.

Dust a work surface with flour. Roll out the dough quite thinly to make a large rectangle measuring at least 30 x 40cm. The pastry will be flecked with squashed butter and this is exactly how it should look.

Cut the pastry in half and put one piece on top of the other. Cut in half again and do the same thing. Repeat one more time so you end up with 8 layers. Very lightly roll the pastry to bring the layers together, then cut it in half and wrap.

Store the pastry until you need to use it. It will keep in the fridge for a week, or in the freezer for up to 3 months.

If you want to make sweet rough puff pastry, add a tablespoon of caster sugar to the flour.

Lemon & elderflower biscuits

Makes 24

100g caster sugar
1 tbsp elderflower cordial
zest of 1 lemon
125g butter
pinch of salt
1 egg
250g plain flour

These are perfect with the gooseberry fool on page 238.

Mix the caster sugar with the cordial so it is the texture of wet sand. Beat this mixture with the lemon zest, butter and a pinch of salt until soft and fluffy. Add the egg and plain flour and mix as briefly as possible to make a smooth dough.

Divide the mixture in half and roll each piece into a log of about 5–6cm in diameter. Wrap and chill for at least an hour. You can keep the logs in the fridge for up to a week in a sealed container or freeze them, until you are ready to bake the biscuits.

To bake the biscuits, preheat the oven to 180°C/Fan 160°C/Gas 4. Line 2 baking trays with baking parchment.

Slice each log into 12 rounds and arrange them on the baking trays. Bake in the preheated oven for about 12 minutes until the biscuits are cooked through and light golden brown in colour. Remove from the oven and carefully transfer them to a rack to cool. Store in an airtight container.

Fudge

Makes about 25 squares

1 x 397g can of condensed milk
125ml milk
200g demerara sugar
250g light brown soft sugar
125g butter, diced
2 tsp vanilla extract

Line a 20cm square tin with baking parchment.

Put all the ingredients in a large saucepan. Slowly heat, stirring constantly, until the sugar has dissolved and the butter has melted. Turn up the heat and bring the mixture to the boil, stirring regularly and thoroughly to make sure it doesn't catch on the bottom of the pan or around the edges.

If you have a sugar thermometer, keep boiling the mixture until it reaches 115–116°C. If you don't have a sugar thermometer, you can use the 'soft ball' test. Have a bowl of cold water ready and drop a little of the mixture into it – it should set to a soft, pliable ball. The fudge normally takes about 10 minutes to reach this stage, but to be on the safe side, start testing after 8 minutes – you don't want your fudge to go beyond this point as it will become very hard.

Remove the pan from the heat and leave to cool for 10 minutes. Using electric beaters or the paddle on a stand mixer, beat the fudge as it cools. It will thicken as it does so and should change from very glossy to more of a matt appearance. It should also go very slightly grainy.

Keep beating until the mixture has cooled to about 60°C, then transfer to the prepared tin and spread it as evenly as possible – a wet palette knife helps with this. Leave to cool and set. When the fudge is firm, cut into cubes and store in an airtight container. It will keep best in the fridge.

Proper custard

Serves 4-6

250ml whole milk
250ml double cream
1 vanilla pod, split, or
    1 tsp vanilla extract
1 coffee bean (optional)
6 egg yolks
50g caster sugar

Put the milk and cream in a pan with the vanilla pod or extract and the coffee bean, if using (it adds depth of flavour but doesn't make the custard taste of coffee). Bring the milk and cream almost to the boil, then remove the pan from the heat and set it aside for the flavours to infuse while the mixture cools.

Whisk the egg yolks and sugar together in a bowl until pale and foamy. Reheat the milk and cream to just below boiling point. Strain the milk mixture through a sieve into a jug and rinse out the saucepan. Slowly pour the milk mixture over the eggs, whisking constantly as you do so, then pour it all back into the saucepan. Set the pan over a very low heat and stir constantly until the custard has thickened slightly and you can draw a line through it and it coats the back of a spoon.

Strain the custard again and if you aren't serving it immediately, put the vanilla pod, if using, back into it. Cover the custard with cling film, making sure it comes into contact with the surface of the custard to prevent a skin from forming. Leave to cool.

Vegetable stock

Makes about 1.5 litres

1 tsp olive oil
2 large onions, roughly chopped
3 large carrots, chopped
200g squash or pumpkin,
    unpeeled, diced
4 celery sticks, sliced
2 leeks, sliced
100ml white wine or vermouth
large thyme sprig
large parsley sprig
1 bay leaf
a few peppercorns

Heat the olive oil in a large saucepan. Add all the vegetables and fry them over a high heat, stirring regularly, until they start to brown and caramelise around the edges. This will take at least 10 minutes. Add the white wine or vermouth and boil until it has evaporated away.

Cover the vegetables with 2 litres of water and add the herbs and peppercorns. Bring to the boil, then turn the heat down to a gentle simmer. Cook the stock, uncovered, for about an hour, stirring every so often.

Strain the stock through a colander lined with muslin or kitchen paper into a bowl. Store it in the fridge for up to a week or freeze it.

Fish stock

Makes about 1.5 litres

1.5kg fish heads and bones
    from white fish (ask your
    fishmonger)
1 tbsp salt
2 tbsp olive oil
1 onion, finely chopped
2 leeks, finely sliced
½ fennel bulb, finely chopped
1 celery stick, sliced
2 garlic cloves, sliced
200ml white wine
bouquet garni (made up of
    2 sprigs each of parsley,
    tarragon and thyme)
2 bay leaves
a few peppercorns
1 piece of thinly pared lemon zest

Put the fish heads and bones in a bowl, cover them with cold water and add the salt. Leave to stand for an hour, then drain them and wash thoroughly under running water. This process helps to draw out any blood from the fish and gives you a much clearer, fresher-tasting stock.

Heat the olive oil in a large saucepan. Add the onion, leeks, fennel, celery and garlic. Cook the vegetables over a medium heat for several minutes until they start to soften without taking on any colour.

Add the fish heads and bones and pour over the wine. Bring to the boil, then add 2 litres of water. Bring back to the boil, skim off any mushroom-coloured foam that appears on the surface, then turn the heat down to a very slow simmer. Add the herbs, peppercorns and lemon zest and leave to simmer for 30 minutes, skimming off any foam every so often.

Strain the stock through a colander or sieve into a bowl, then line the sieve with muslin or kitchen paper and strain the stock again. Don't push it through as that will result in a cloudier stock. Leave to cool, then keep in the fridge for 3–4 days or freeze it.

Chicken stock

Makes about 1 litre

at least 1 chicken carcass, pulled
    apart
4 chicken wings (optional)
1 onion, unpeeled, cut into
    quarters
1 large carrot, cut into large
    chunks
2 celery sticks, roughly chopped
1 leek, roughly chopped
1 tsp black peppercorns
3 bay leaves
large parsley sprig
small thyme sprig
a few garlic cloves, unpeeled
    (optional)

Put the chicken bones and the wings, if using, into a saucepan that's just large enough for all the chicken to fit quite snugly. Cover with cold water, bring to the boil, then skim off any foam that collects. Add the remaining ingredients and turn the heat down to a very low simmer. Partially cover the pan with a lid.

Leave the stock to simmer for about 3 hours, then remove the pan from the heat. Strain the stock through a colander lined with muslin or kitchen paper into a bowl.

The stock can be used right away, although it is best to skim off most of the fat that will collect on the top. If you don't need the stock immediately, leave it to cool. The fat will set on top and will be much easier to remove.

You can keep the stock in the fridge for up to 5 days, or freeze it. If you want to make a larger amount of stock, save up your chicken carcasses in the freezer or add more chicken wings.

Beef stock

Makes about 2 litres

1.5kg beef bones, including
    marrow bones if possible,
    cut into small lengths
500g piece of beef shin or any
    cheap, fairly lean cut
2 onions, unpeeled, roughly
    chopped
1 leek, roughly chopped
2 celery sticks, roughly chopped
2 carrots, roughly chopped
2 tomatoes
½ tsp peppercorns
bouquet garni made up of large
    sprigs of thyme, parsley and
    2 bay leaves

Put the beef bones and meat into a large saucepan and cover them with cold water – you'll need at least 3–3.5 litres. Bring the water to the boil and when a starchy, mushroom-grey foam appears, start skimming. Keep on skimming as the foam turns white and continue until it has almost stopped developing.

Add the vegetables, peppercorns and bouquet garni, turn down the heat until the stock is simmering very gently, then partially cover the pan with a lid. Leave to simmer for 3–4 hours.

Line a colander with 2 layers of muslin or kitchen paper and place it over a large bowl. Ladle the stock into the sieve or colander to strain it. Remove the meat and set it aside, then discard everything else. Pour the strained stock into a large container and leave it to cool. The fat should solidify on top of the stock and will be very easy to remove. You can keep the stock in the fridge for 2 or 3 days or freeze it.

Don't chuck out the piece of meat – it's good in sandwiches or can be sliced, fried and added to salads.

Index

W

Y

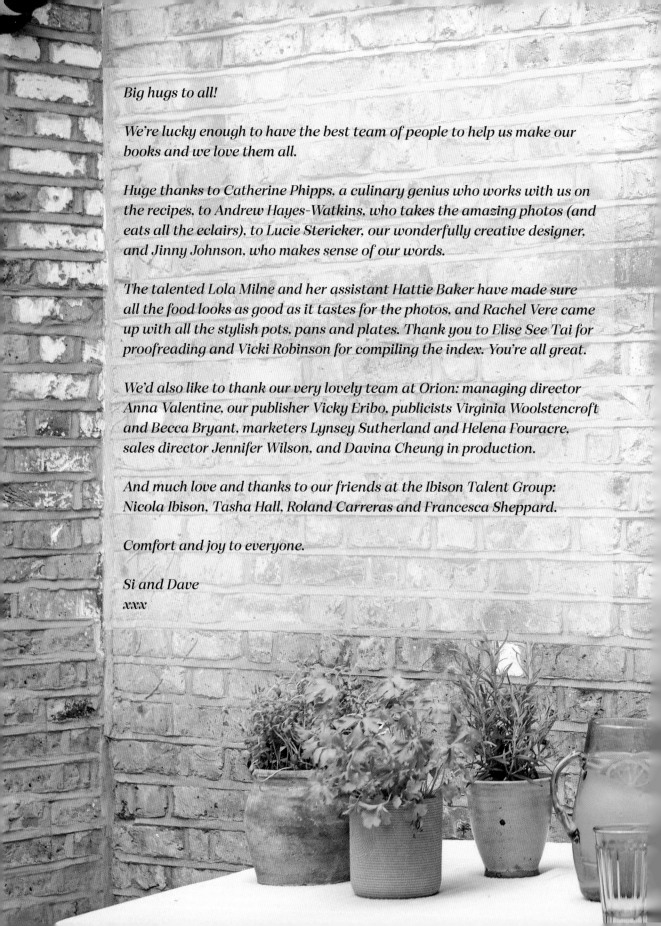

Big hugs to all!

We're lucky enough to have the best team of people to help us make our books and we love them all.

Huge thanks to Catherine Phipps, a culinary genius who works with us on the recipes, to Andrew Hayes-Watkins, who takes the amazing photos (and eats all the eclairs), to Lucie Stericker, our wonderfully creative designer, and Jinny Johnson, who makes sense of our words.

The talented Lola Milne and her assistant Hattie Baker have made sure all the food looks as good as it tastes for the photos, and Rachel Vere came up with all the stylish pots, pans and plates. Thank you to Elise See Tai for proofreading and Vicki Robinson for compiling the index. You're all great.

We'd also like to thank our very lovely team at Orion: managing director Anna Valentine, our publisher Vicky Eribo, publicists Virginia Woolstencroft and Becca Bryant, marketers Lynsey Sutherland and Helena Fouracre, sales director Jennifer Wilson, and Davina Cheung in production.

And much love and thanks to our friends at the Ibison Talent Group: Nicola Ibison, Tasha Hall, Roland Carreras and Francesca Sheppard.

Comfort and joy to everyone.

Si and Dave
xxx

Dave: I'd like to dedicate this book to the hospital team who have cared for me over the last eighteen months. It's because of them that I'm here today and able to continue cooking and enjoying comforting food.

Si: To my sons and to Ada Grace, my gorgeous granddaughter, who has brought joy, laughter and a new generation to the King family. And to Nicole Kavanagh for her constant support and guidance through life's trials and tribulations.

First published in Great Britain in 2023 by Seven Dials,
an imprint of The Orion Publishing Group Ltd
Carmelite House, 50 Victoria Embankment
London EC4Y 0DZ

An Hachette UK Company

13 5 7 9 10 8 6 4 2

Text copyright © Bytebrook Limited and Sharpletter Limited 2023
Design and layout copyright © Seven Dials 2023

ISBN (Hardback): 978 1 3996 0730 8
ISBN (eBook): 978 1 3996 0731 5

Publisher: Vicky Eribo
Editor: Jinny Johnson
Recipe consultant: Catherine Phipps
Photography: Andrew Hayes-Watkins
Design & art direction: Lucie Stericker, Studio 7:15
Food stylist: Lola Milne
Food stylist's assistant: Hattie Baker
Prop stylist: Rachel Vere
Proofreader: Elise See Tai
Indexer: Vicki Robinson
Senior production controller: Davina Cheung

Cover design: Jessica Hart

Origination by F1 Colour Ltd., London

Printed in Italy

MIX
Paper | Supporting responsible forestry
FSC® C023419
www.fsc.org

More best-sellers from the Hairy Bikers